GUIDE TO A WELL-BEHAVED CAT

CAT

A Sound Approach to Cat Training

Phil Maggitti

BARRON'S

All inquiries should be addressed to:
Barron's Educational Series, Inc.
250 Wireless Boulevard
Hauppauge, New York 11788

International Standard Book No. 0-8120-1476-6

Library of Congress Catalog Card No. 93-8751

Library of Congress Cataloging-in-Publication Data

Maggitti, Phil.
    Guide to a well-behaved cat: a sound approach to cat training / Phil Maggitti.
       p.   cm.
    Includes index.
    ISBN 0-8120-1476-6
    1. Cats—Training. 2. Cats. I. Title.
    SF446.6.M34   1993
    636.8'0887—dc20   93-8751
                                                   CIP
PRINTED IN HONG KONG

56   9927   98765432

Photo Credits:

Animals Limited: front cover, back cover; Brian Blauser: pages 10, 11, 25, 50, 71; Carlo Carnevali: page 24; Chanan: pages 36, 40, 107; Donna J. Coss: inside front cover, inside back cover, pages 7, 18, 38, 61, 75, 78, 79 (bottom), 80, 85, 98, 102, 115, 135; Michael Kobert: pages 2, 29, 42, 44, 46, 48, 49, 61, 87, 89; Phil Maggitti: pages 12, 13, 23, 52, 77, 83, 86, 91, 96, 101, 103, 105, 111, 113, 124; Phil Segura: page 127; Larry Sherman: page 79 (top); Judy Strom: pages 62, 73, 116, 118.

About the Author:

Phil Maggitti is a freelance writer and editor living in southeastern Pennsylvania. He has published more than 250 articles about cats in a variety of periodicals. He is the author of *Scottish Fold Cats* and the editor of a bimonthly cat magazine. Mr. Maggitti is also a former contributing editor to *Spur*, a magazine devoted to Thoroughbreds and country living, and to *The Animals' Agenda*, an animal-rights and ecology magazine. He has received several awards from the American Horse Council for his writing, including best feature article and best personal column. Mr. Maggitti and his wife Mary Ann live with nine cats, most of them foundlings, and four pug dogs.

Important Note:

When you handle cats, you may sometimes get scratched or bitten. If this happens, have a doctor treat the injuries immediately.

Make sure your cat receives all the necessary shots and dewormings, otherwise serious danger to the animal and to human health may arise. A few diseases and parasites can be communicated to humans. If your cat shows any signs of illness, you should consult a veterinarian. If you are worried about your own health, see your doctor and tell him or her that you have cats.

Some people have allergic reactions to cats. If you think you might be allergic, see your doctor before you get a cat.

It is possible for a cat to cause damage to someone else's property and even to cause accidents. For your own protection you should make sure your insurance covers such eventualities, and you definitely should have liability insurance.

Contents

Acknowledgments

The following people helped to make this a better book: Nancy Kobert, Kathryn Segura, and Cristie Miele, all of whom train animals professionally and all of whom demonstrated that the patience required by their profession is also required when talking with some writers; Daniel Q. Estep, PhD, and Suzanne Hetts, PhD, certified applied animal behaviorists, who helped me to sort myth from sound methodology in explaining how to modify a cat's behavior; Helgard Niewisch, DVM, who evaluated and fine tuned the manuscript for Barron's; Don Reis, senior editor at Barron's, who was most patient in nudging the manuscript along when nudging was in order; Fred Reifsnyder, who helped with the grooming chapter and the training photos; my wife Mary Ann who proofread, provided moral support, and made many helpful suggestions, and who is most tolerant of eccentricities in her cats and in her husband's working schedule; and our four pug dogs, who set a good example for our nine cats by always coming when called.

Preface

Anyone who presumes to write a book about cat training must produce either an unavoidably slim volume, scarcely longer than a pamphlet, or a book that contains a number of chapters devoted to topics entirely unrelated to cat training: chapters about traveling with cats, breeding cats, and so on.

Guide to a Well-behaved Cat attempts to avoid both these approaches. Obviously, it is longer than a booklet, and even though it contains a few nontraining chapters, those chapters are related to —and crucial to—the training process because they provide background information about the cat's evolution and domestication and their effects on feline personality. This information is meaningful to anyone who attempts to train a cat. Just as the best teachers and coaches are those who understand their subjects, the best cat trainers are those who understand cats. Therefore, the more you understand your cat, the more you will enjoy it. The better you comprehend your cat's needs, desires, and instincts, the better able you will be to train it.

Training cats begins with the indisputable observation that a cat is not a dog and should not be expected to behave like one. "Cats, unlike dogs, are not amused by, nor do they in any way take any interest in, what are termed *tricks,"* wrote British cat fancier Harrison Weir more than one hundred years ago. And cats have changed little since Weir made that observation.

Cats can be trained to come when they are called, most of the time, to walk on a lead, to jump through hoops, to retrieve thrown objects, and to perform other tricks—if that is important to you. Chances are, however, that such activities will not be as important to your cat, nor will they be performed by a cat as readily and as cheerfully as they will be performed by a dog. If you covet that sort of prewired obedience and willing performance in a pet, perhaps you should have a dog as well as—or instead of—a cat. If you think that training your cat will add a dimension to your relationship that is pleasant and rewarding for both of you, this book will help to facilitate that training.

Phil Maggitti
Summer, 1993

Chapter 1
Evolution of the Cat

With explosive grace that calls to mind the tiger, a cat bounds across the living room, feet scarcely touching the rug. A smooth, sinewy impulse carries him easily onto a deep windowsill, where he crouches with murderous intent and stares with age-old malice at a bird sitting in a tree outside the window. While the bird warbles cheerfully, the cat bristles with instinctive intent. Given the chance, he would reduce that bird to a blizzard of feathers.

Outside, a neighbor's cat is watching the bird, too, and begins to slink toward the tree. The bird, spying the cat's motion, flies quickly away.

The cat in the window jumps to the floor, races to a plump, stuffed chair, and furiously sinks the claws of one front paw, then the other, into the side of the chair over and over again. The cat's mistress walks into the room and shouts, "No, Toby. No." But Toby pummels the chair several times before scampering down a hallway.

"I'll never understand that cat," the woman sighs. "I don't know why he won't use the scratching post in the den."

If looks could kill, this bird would be an endangered species.

To understand our friend the cat, we must begin our study in lands too ancient to imagine, in times too distant to comprehend. We must consider the evolution of the cat, its solitary habits, and the circumstances attending its domestication. We must follow, for the most part, a faint, whispering trail through shifting sands. What's more, we are apt to return with questions in place of answers and with theories instead of solutions. Thousands of scientific and popular articles describing feline behavior have been written, but despite all this microscopic and oftentimes intrusive investigation, no one has yet demonstrated with certitude whether cats sit on our laps because they want warmth or affection—or both.

Taxonomy of the Cat Kingdom: Animal

Like all living things, *Felis catus,* the domestic cat, is classified according to the kingdom, phylum, class, order, family, genus, and species to which it belongs. Domestic cats are members of the animal kingdom, which is principally populated by many-celled organ-

When a house-cat looks in the mirror, this is what it sees: a portrait of the swiftness, grace, and agility that are the hallmarks of all cats great or small.

isms that have a well-defined shape, are usually limited in terms of growth, are able to move voluntarily, possess sensory and nervous systems that allow them to respond rapidly to stimuli, and must acquire and digest ready-to-eat food because they are incapable of synthesizing their own food from inorganic (nonliving) material.

Phylum: Chordata (Subphylum: Vertebrata)

Cats belong to the phylum Chordata, the most advanced in the animal kingdom. All chordates possess gill clefts (or pouches) and a notochord at some point in their embryonic development. (A notochord is a long, flexible, rod-shaped structure that supports the vertical axis of the body.) Vertebrates, in addition, have segmented backbones, a brain enclosed in a cranium, one heart, two simple eyes, two kidneys, two pairs of limbs, and a closed blood system.

Class: Mammalia (Subclass: Eutheria)

Cats, like other members of the class Mammalia, are hairy, warm-blooded, possess four-chambered hearts, and suckle their young. The most familiar mammals, cats included, are found in the mammalian subclass Eutheria, whose young are born structurally complete following a period of gestation during which they develop inside an internal nest, the womb, which is functionally analogous to an egg.

Eutherian embryos obtain food and oxygen from their mothers via an umbilical cord. Most eutherians develop a set of milk or deciduous teeth that are replaced eventually by permanent teeth.

Order: Carnivora

The cat's all-meat diet, its claws, and its canine teeth mark it as a thorough-going carnivore.

Family: Felidae

Like other members of the Felidae family, the cat has whiskers, slit irises, and the ability to retract its claws into its pads.

Genus: *Felis*

The cat's slender body and its dentition pattern are distinguishing characteristics of its genus, *Felis.*

Species: *Catus*

Its domesticated status and its line of descent—from the African and European wild cats—have earned the domesticated cat its species name, *catus.*

Before There Were Cats

Precambrian Time

Scientists organize the awesome sweep of the Earth's geological history into two major time divisions: Precambrian and Cambrian. The Precambrian division, which began with the formation of the Earth more than 4.6 billion years ago, comprises the first 4.1 billion years (roughly 89 percent) of the Earth's existence. Because virtually no fossils remain from Precambrian time, it also is called Cryptozoic, meaning "hidden life."

That hidden life began in the seas about 3.5 billion years ago with the appearance of one-celled organisms that belonged to the kingdom Monera, which includes bacteria, blue-green algae, and primitive pathogens. By 700 million years ago, the first marine invertebrates (animals lacking backbones) had evolved. The most familiar invertebrates are sponges, corals, and mollusks.

Cambrian Time

The Cambrian time division, which began 570 million years ago, is divided into three eras: the Paleozoic, the Mesozoic, and the Cenozoic. These eras are subdivided into periods and epochs.

The Earth's climate had grown warmer by the beginning of the Cambrian time division, and oxygen had become present in significant amounts in the atmosphere, but life did not make its way onto land until the Silurian period, 430 to 395 million years ago. The first land-going pioneers included simple plants, which had vascular systems for circulating water, and scorpionlike animals that resembled marine arthropods.

The earliest primitive mammals, fellow members of the class to which cats belong, appeared during the Triassic period, 225 to 195 million years ago. These mammals were no larger than a cat and no smaller than a shrew. During this same period, dinosaurs began roaming the Earth.

The Cat's Distant Ancestors

Carnivores, the members of the order to which cats belong, first appeared during the Eocene epoch, which lasted from 54 to 38 million years ago. All carnivores alive today are descended from miacids, a group of small, slender, longtailed, forest-dwelling, tree-climbing animals with retractable claws. Miacids flourished about 45 million B.C. Before they became extinct, they had evolved into two suborders: the Pinnipedia and the Fissipedia. Pinnipeds are animals whose limbs are flattened into flippers. Fissipeds, so named because they have separated toes, include dogs, wolves, bears, weasels, cats, hyenas, and civets.

Felidae, the family to which cats belong, is believed to have evolved during the Eocene epoch, but the oldest fossil remains that have been identified positively as felid date from the subsequent Oligocene epoch, 38 to 26 million years ago. One of the most epic felids was the saber-toothed tiger, a hulking, fearsome hunter that could bring down an elephant. Saber-tooths ranged—

pretty much at will, one suspects—throughout Europe, Asia, Africa, North America, and, subsequently, South America. For millions of years before they became extinct, they shared the Earth with smaller, faster, less toothsome, but more intelligent felines.

The oldest fossils that exhibit close similarities to today's cats are roughly 12 million years old. Their age places them at the beginning of the Pliocene epoch, 12 million to 2.5 million years ago. This is thought to be the period when the earliest ancestors of modern-day cats started to develop as a separate genus.

The Felidae Clan

Zoologists disagree regarding the number of genera into which Felidae or felids should be divided. Some zoologists prefer three genera. *Panthera* includes cats that can roar—the lion, tiger, leopard, snow leopard, clouded leopard, and jaguar. These cats are able to roar because of the flexibility of their partially cartilaginous hyoid bones. The hyoids are a paired chain of small bones, found at the base of the tongue, that connects the larynx with the skull.

Most zoologists assign all non-roaring cats but the cheetah to the genus *Felis*. Members of this genus are commonly called small cats, although *Felis concolor,* the puma, is as big as a leopard. The cheetah, because its claws are not fully retractable, occupies it own genus, *Acinonyx.*

Some zoologists divide cats into more than three genera. The clouded leopard, for example, is now and then awarded its own genus, *Neofelis,* because it has exceptionally long upper canine teeth. Lynxes, which have short tails and tufted ears, sometimes rate their own genus, *Lynx.* Ocelots and Geoffroy's cats, because they have 36 chromosomes instead of the felid's customary 38, are occasionally put into a separate genus, *Leopardus.*

Zoologists also disagree regarding the number of feline species. Again, the disagreement results from differences of opinion over what characteristics are important enough to warrant separate classification. Whether one reckons 35, 38, or some other number of small-cat species, they are more plentiful than are the species of large cats. Indeed, there are but seven large cats: the lion, tiger, leopard, snow leopard, clouded leopard, jaguar, and cheetah.

Size and nomenclature notwithstanding, each member of the Felidae family is an exquisitely specialized hunter, feeding almost entirely on meat and almost exclusively on vertebrates. And all Felidae—except the lion and the cheetah—are creatures of solitary inclination.

Felis Silvestris and Friends

The cat's adaptability is perhaps its most impressive trait. Except for Antarctica and Australia, in which native-born cats have never existed, the entire world has been the cat's stage. Cats have colonized every manner of environment from scorched deserts to sheer mountains to luxuriant tropical forests. Unfortunately, the cat's talent for adaptation virtually precludes identifying with any accuracy the original habitat of the ancestors from which modern-day cats are descended.

Nevertheless, the Italian biologist Eugenia Natoli declared in *Cats of the World* that the forebears of today's domestic cat began to evolve at least two million years ago. Their evolution led to the emergence of the genus *Felis* as a distinct branch of the class Felidae. *Felis catus,* the species to which modern cats belong, did not begin to evolve, according to Natoli, until five thousand years ago when humans first domesticated *Felis silvestris,* the wild cat from which today's house cats descended.

Most researchers believe that the African wild cat, *Felis libyca* or sometimes *Felis silvestris libyca,* is the probable ancestor of the domestic cat. A yellow, mutedly striped, slightly larger than domestic size feline, the African wild cat is found primarily in deserts throughout

Africa, Syria, Arabia, and parts of India.

There are almost as many reasons as a cat has lives for assuming that African wild cats are the fathers and mothers of domestic house cats. Chief among these reasons are correlations between human and feline habitats during the period when cats were most likely domesticated, the physical characteristics of mummified cats found in Egypt, adaptations in the domestic cat, including a hearing apparatus suited to open spaces like the desert, and behavioral evidence, namely, the docile nature of African wild cats. In fact, these cats often live and forage near human settlements today; and visitors to Africa have observed natives catching and rearing young wild cats, which behave, when mature, much the way domestic cats behave.

In addition to the physiological and behavioral evidence suggesting that the African wild cat is the principal ancestor of *Felis catus,* there is etymological testimony as well. *Kadiz,* the Nubian word for cat, sounds remarkably like the word for cat in the following languages: English, *cat;* French, *chat;* German, *Katze;* Spanish, *gato;* fourth-century Latin, *catus;* and modern Arabic, *quttah.*

The Nubian language was spoken in parts of the Sudan and in the Nile River valley. Most researchers agree that the cat was domesticated in Egypt (see Domestication of the Cat, page 12). Therefore, it is not surprising that the word for cat in several other languages appears to have been derived from the Nubian *kadiz.* Moreover, the word *Pasht*—another name for Bastet, the Egyptian cat goddess—resembles the English diminutive puss and the Romanian word for cat, *pisicca.*

Following their domestication, cats became the cat's meow in Egypt, where a cat cult became identified with Bast, sometimes called Bastet, the goddess of maternity and fertility. Because of the high status they occupied in Egypt, where their export was severely restricted, domesticated cats were slow to appear in other countries. Cats were brought to Europe, but not in large numbers, from Imperial Roman times onward, wrote zoologist F.E.

About 3,600 years ago, a cat cult in Egypt became identified with Bast, the goddess of maternity, fertility, and other traditional feminine virtues. Bast also was known as Pasht, which is thought to be the word from which puss was derived.

Zeuner in *A History of Domesticated Animals.* The Romans introduced cats throughout the farthest parts of their empire, including England, where cats arrived between 300 and 500 A.D. The Romans also introduced cats to central Europe.

Though *Felis catus* most likely descended from the African wild cat, some observers believe that at least one other species influenced the development of domestic cats. Claire Necker—former museum curator, naturalist, and author of *The Natural History of Cats*—is one of many people who theorize that the first domesticated descendants of the African wild cat hybridized with the European wild cat, *Felis silvestris,* thereby providing modern-day cats with a mixed genetic ancestry.

Originally found from northern Europe to the Caucasus and Asia Minor, the European wild cat is confined mostly to a few areas of Scotland today. A fierce, intractable, forest-dwelling cat adept at tree climbing and living in dense vegetation, *F. silvestris* possibly contributed darker tabby markings and a certain fiery spirit to the lightly marked and more docile cats descended from African wild cats. (Some people believe that a northern Asian cat, *Felis manul,* may have contributed to the development of today's longhaired cats. Felis manul is also called Pallas' cat or the steppe cat.)

The Cat Who Walks by Himself

The oldest known fossil remains that have been identified positively as belonging to a member of the Felidae family date from the Oligocene epoch, 38 to 26 million years ago. The earliest fossil remains positively identified as Hominidae, the family to which we humans belong, are four million years old. *Homo,* our anatomically correct genus, did not evolve until 2.5 million years ago; and *sapiens,* our species, is but 400,000 years old. The long interval between the emergence of the forebears of today's domestic cat and our own forebears provided the cat with plenty of time to become set in its ways. Those ways were the most solitary of any animal domesticated by human beings.

Who can blame a cat for being self-involved? It is hard to be otherwise when you are this handsome.

All animals domesticated before the cat—dogs, reindeer, yaks, and pigs among them—had lived in some kind of communal arrangement on which their biological and social well-being depended. They also exhibited several highly significant predictors of domestication: membership in a large social group, an acquaintance with a hierarchial group structure, omnivorous eating habits, adaptability to a wide range of environments, limited agility, the use of movements or posturing to advertise sexual receptivity, and a promiscuous lifestyle. The cat, bless its singular heart, lights up the scoreboard on only three of these traits: sexual posturing, promiscuity, and adaptability to a wide range of environments.

The ability—in truth, the need—to function in and to accept one's place in a tightly structured group contributes more than any other characteristic to ease of domestication and to an animal's attachment to the domesticating species. This trait further explains, by its absence, why the cat does not regard humans with the same incessant affection as the dog or the same patient stoicism as the horse. These species follow the lead of the dominant member of the herd or pack, usually the alpha female. In an equine herd, for example, when the alpha mare stops to graze, the herd stops, too. When the mare takes off at a gallop, the herd follows. When the mare decides to rest, the herd settles down as well.

In addition to a willingness to follow their leader's example, animals that are members of a highly structured group develop better communication systems than do solitary animals because social interactions are important to the pack dweller's survival. If two feral dogs living in a pack have an altercation, they need a way of reconciling their differences because eventually they will have to go hunting with their pack. That is one reason why canine communication systems and social-interaction patterns allow dogs to reach a settlement much more easily than cats will do. Cats do not need to hunt together. They have the luxury of bearing grudges if they like.

The pack dweller's centuries-old, follow-the-leader instinct predisposes Trigger and Lassie to accept humans as the top dogs in their lives; but no such instinct prevails upon Garfield, who kept his own hours and his own counsel for thousands of centuries before signing a series of one-generation-only contracts to do light mouse work for humans. Therefore, the dog is prewired to seek the good will of the alpha human, but the cat is inclined to offer its friendship to such as deserve it.

Furthermore, the interval since the cat was first domesticated is but a blink in time's steady gaze. And, as Zeuner has remarked, cats are still in the first blush of domestication. They are entirely capable of reverting to—and surviving in—a feral state. Domestication has modified

patterns have observed cats that have been identified as occupying adjacent territories getting together to socialize for an evening. Their gatherings usually occur at a meeting place not far from the cats' home ranges. Mutual grooming and licking are part of the program, which lasts several hours. Cats then repair to their individual sleeping quarters back home on their ranges. If they meet by chance the following day, they might not be so affable as they were the night before.

Although cats do not establish fixed social hierarchies, they do get together to socialize on occasion.

them but little vis-a-vis their distant ancestors.

Jill Mellen, PhD, research coordinator at the Washington Park Zoo in Portland, Oregon, believes those ancestors exerted a greater effect on the cat's personality than did the circumstances in which the cat was domesticated by our ancestors (see Domestication of the Cat, page 12). "The dog's ancestors were wolves, which are highly social individuals," says Mellen. "Cats are not social at all. This doesn't mean they don't have a social life or that they don't interact with one another. It means they're solitary hunters. It's not adaptive for cats to live in large groups because they eat small rodents."

Thus, feral cats are never seen having a communal supper around a mouse. But neither are cats the lone wolves that conventional wisdom makes them out to be. Researchers studying cats' behavior

Why Cats Walk with Us

No animal has had more unfortunate press than the cat. Deified during the Egyptian empire, vilified in the High Middle Ages, romanticized by everyone from Lewis Carroll to Ernest Hemingway, the cat remains grievously misunderstood for being so frequently misrepresented. Neither demon nor deity, and certainly not the haughty curmudgeon that some cartoonists and a few retrograde feature writers would have us believe, the cat deserves a more measured interpretation.

Though many feline myths warrant exposure, let the record show, nevertheless, that cats as a race are not exceedingly sly, enigmatic, arrogant, remote, ethereal, intimidating, or all that terribly complex. Nor were they created so that humans might caress the tiger. A cat is nobody's stand-in. And for all their quiet sovereignty—not to mention their seeming inclination to do what they wish while getting what they want—cats are quite willing to dance attendance on our comings and goings as if they were front-page news. The cats' dance, however, is a minuet, not a polka. Their song a chanson, not an anthem. Their poetry a lyric, not an epic. And while they are capable of playing the clown, they are quick to repair any snags in their dignity.

Despite their reputation for being aloof, cats are inclined to treat virtually every strange vertebrate they meet as a fellow cat—as long as that vertebrate does not trigger a cat's hunting instincts by making the rustling, squeaking, or scratching sounds that spell *p-r-e-y* to a cat. Therefore, absent any unpleasant experiences with humankind, cats are wont to regard the people they meet as fellow cats, too.

Because we bring out the children in cats, and they in us, cats form closer relationships with humans than they do with other members of their own species.

Indeed, wrote German zoologist Paul Leyhausen in *Cat Behavior,* cats generally form closer bonds with humans than with other cats.

Leyhausen, who kept scores of cats for systematic, day-to-day observation, believed that cats housed together in large numbers, either for research or for breeding purposes, could not satisfy their social needs by contact with one another. He also believed that cats living as house pets needed human contact, too.

Leyhausen puzzled over the fact that cats which shunned or fought with other cats in the wild still retained the capacity for close relationships with humans. He theorized that juvenile habits in mammals do not disappear altogether. They are merely suppressed by other, adult activities and may reappear occasionally in the adult animal.

The adult activities that suppress the expression of juvenile habits include guarding territory, rearing young, fighting with rival cats, and seeking opportunities to mate. These activities, said Leyhausen, are so powerful in the adult cat that the inclination to juvenile activities is seldom expressed once a cat reaches maturity. This inclination, however infrequently it finds expression, might nevertheless be the catalyst for what little sociability there is among adult felines, Leyhausen concluded.

For their part, people are congenial enough in the eyes of a cat to merit a social relationship. Cat owners who understand this tendency and who take the time cultivate it, said Leyhausen, may be able to inspire and even rejuvenate a cat's inclination for kittenish behavior. Humans do not raise a cat's hackles the way another cat will; and humans are, as a result, privileged to enjoy the sort of genuine, lasting friendship that seldom occurs between two solitary, free-roaming cats.

The cat's willingness to confer greater friendship on us than on members of its own species is flattering in the extreme. It is also meaningful in the extreme to those who would train a cat or simply share a home with one. The lesson to be learned from the cat's gift of friendship is this: The person who would train a cat must first take the time to become that cat's friend.

Every child should have a cat in which to confide.

A Few Words about Pronouns

During the last decade America became pronoun conscious. The centuries-old practice of using masculine pronouns to refer to all people—men and women—as a group was pronounced sexist.

Eventually these changes became expected of animal writers, too. No longer is it acceptable to refer to cats by the all-purpose "he" no matter what their gender.

In an effort to comply with changing customs in usage, while maintaining at the same time a respect for smoothness of expression, I have decided, for the most part, to use the masculine pronoun when referring to animals in odd-numbered chapters and to use the feminine pronoun in even-numbered chapters. (I arrived at this sequence impartially by flipping a coin.) The neuter pronoun "it" will also appear occasionally when the sex of the animal to which "it" refers is unknown. I apologize to anyone who is offended by that usage, but there comes a point when good writing takes precedence over good politics.

Chapter 2

Domestication of the Cat

Several myths explain the creation of the cat. In one narrative, Apollo, the god of light, music, and poetry, decides to create the lion in order to frighten his sister Diana, goddess of the moon, childbirth, and forests. Scornful of Apollo's effort to intimidate her, Diana responds by creating the cat to mock her brother.

According to another fable, the animals on Noah's Ark become restless and bored a few days after the ark has set sail. As shipmates are wont to do on a cruise, a monkey talks a lioness into a spot of dalliance, which diversion later produces a cat.

A third myth describes how the devil created mice—after God had created the world—in order to destroy the world's crops. God, therefore, created cats to destroy the devil's mice.

The Tabby-Come-Lately

Theories explaining when and where the cat was domesticated are not so fanciful as the myths regarding the cat's creation. Yet many domestication theories are scarcely less difficult to prove.

"About 3,000 B.C." is a commonly quoted estimate of that fortunate dawn when cats began to associate with humankind. A frequently cited backdrop for this event is Egypt. Having noted this, however, we must also note—along with Jill Mellen of the Washington Park Zoo—that "there are probably as many [domestication] theories as there are people who have thought and written about the subject. Unfortunately, the information that would allow us to make more positive statements about

A kitten is a wondrous creation. A winsome notion in a soft, delicate wrapper. A recurring miracle no less miraculous for all its frequency.

when and where the cat was domesticated does not exist. We have the end product—the domesticated cat—but there aren't any domestication secrets locked inside the cat waiting to be discovered."

Most researchers believe that cats are the tabbies-come-lately among domesticated animals, having graduated from the wild no more than five thousand years ago. Others argue that cats were among the first animals to be domesticated and that they were bred for religious sacrifice at least nine thousand years ago. Still others claim the domestic cat is not thoroughly domesticated yet.

According to zoologist F.E. Zeuner, whose authority in such matters is well respected, our ancestors had domesticated at least a dozen animals before striking a bargain with the cat. Domestication began with dogs, reindeer, goats, and sheep during the preagricultural phase, more than ten thousand years ago. Next came the domestication of cattle, buffalo, yaks, and pigs during the early agricultural phase, and of elephants, horses, camels, and mules in various phases thereafter.

Zeuner discounts the notion that cats were domesticated for religious sacrifice. He contends that early humans would have had an easier time obtaining the animals they needed for sacrifice by trapping rather than domesticating them.

Others who have studied ritual sacrifice agree. In a 1986 doctoral dissertation, Mary Christine Rodrigue concluded that ritual sacrifice so complicated human affairs that it could not have been the reason why animals were first domesticated.

Considering these and other judgments—and the cat's vaunted independence—one is inclined to place the cat near the end of the domesticated-animals parade. If one also accepts the theory that cats were domesticated for their skill at catching rats, as many zoologists maintain, one must assume that cats were not domesticated until some time after wheat and barley were first cultivated in the Middle East in the seventh millennium B.C. But how long after is everybody's guess.

Who Domesticated Whom?

Persons seeking to identify the circumstances of the cat's domestication construct their theories from evidence unearthed at ancient

Few of Nature's works are as charming as the young of any species. They stir us to laughter, reduce us to baby talk, and summon from us a tenderness concealed beneath the armor that we wear in our daily confrontations with life.

human settlements and from fragments of early recorded history. Such evidence allows that cats may have been domesticated in several parts of the world simultaneously and that Central Asia and India, both of which were ancient agriculture centers, are possible domestication sites. Yet most observers agree with Italian biologist Eugenia Natoli, who declares that cats were domesticated in ancient Egypt, and who bases her declaration on the thousands of mummified cats that have been discovered there.

Natoli also declared that cats almost certainly were domesticated by Egyptians around 3,000 B.C. But all scholars do not share her dogmatism on this point.

Researchers using carbon-dating techniques estimate that wheat and barley were domesticated in the Middle East in the seventh millennium B.C. Thus, if cats were domesticated because they were useful for protecting grain, they

might have been domesticated earlier than 3,000 B.C.

Bruce Fogle, DVM, MRCVS, and author of *The Cat's Mind,* observes that between 3,000 and 1,600 B.C., the period most researchers cite as the time when cats were first domesticated, cats also achieved cult status in Egypt. Arguing from the premise that cats were unlikely to be revered as soon as they had been domesticated, Fogle suggests that the emergence of cat cults could imply a longstanding, though undocumented, relationship between cats and humans. Therefore, he concludes, cats may have allowed themselves to be domesticated at the time they first saw any advantage in doing so. That is, about the seventh millennium B.C.

Animal behaviorist James A. Serpell agrees that the cat probably was domesticated in Egypt. Yet, Serpell cautions, it is not possible to do more than estimate the time when domestication occurred.

According to Serpell, the earliest pictorial representations of cats in Egypt date from the third millennium B.C., but context does not reveal whether the animals depicted were wild or domestic. A representation of a cat wearing a collar was found in the fifth-dynasty tomb of Ti (circa 2,600 B.C.), yet researchers are not certain whether this was a captive or a domesticated cat. Serpell concludes that from 1,600 B.C. onward, however, the large number of paintings and effigies in which cats were

A cat's idea of heaven is depicted in this Egyptian tomb painting.

featured suggest that cats were fully domesticated by then.

The length of time the cat has been domesticated—be it 3,600 or almost 9,000 years—is not as significant as the length of time (roughly 390,000 years) that passed between the appearance of *Homo sapiens* and the initiation of his compact with the African wild cat. During that interval the cat had all the time in the world to become set in its ways. Those ways include, even to this day, a dignified self-sufficiency and an inclination to greet with disdain any beckoning attempt on the part of humans that is not accompanied by food. Thus, says Zeuner, it is reasonable to conclude that the Egyptian cat was tolerated—and perhaps even fed—without being domesticated by the villagers whose stores of grain she protected from rodents.

There is no evidence, adds zoologist Paul Leyhausen, that humans planned the cat's domestication the way they had planned the domestication of all other animals. True to its independent nature, the cat was a self-domesticating creature. Humans played little more than a supporting role, and a largely unwitting one, in the process.

This laissez-faire doctrine of cat domestication appears credible. It is echoed today by many cat owners who report that their cats adopted them—showing up at the back door one day, staying for dinner and then for good.

Nevertheless, other theories have been advanced to explain the origin of the cat's association with humans. The appearance of cats in hunting scenes in ancient Egyptian art has led some observers to believe that cats were domesticated for their skill in the chase. But if cats were ever used to any large extent for hunting, says Zeuner, they were not used in this capacity for long. And their hunting skills would not have been important enough to justify the effort it would have taken to domesticate cats for hunting. Yet, adds Zeuner, the motivation for domesticating cats was only partly economic. If this is so, another consideration might have been companionship.

The notion that cats domesticated themselves is no doubt gratifying to persons who admire the cat's autonomy, says Serpell. But this theory casts the Egyptians in a strangely passive light. An overriding interest in animals was a hallmark of Egyptian social and religious life. These were the people, remember, for whom animal taming and pet keeping always had been favorite leisure-time activities. It is unlikely, argues Serpell, that after taming monkeys, baboons, hyenas, mongooses, crocodiles, lions, and an assortment of wild ungulates, Egyptians would have neglected cats. The rodent-catching abilities of cats notwithstanding, Serpell believes that Egyptians would have revered cats as cult objects and as household pets whether there was any practical or economic advantage for doing so.

Therefore, some people assume Egyptians may have domesticated the cat by adopting litters of abandoned kittens or by driving off a mother cat and raising her young. The former method of domestication is reenacted today by persons who take in deserted kittens and become their surrogate mothers.

Although most people subscribe to one or the other of the various cat-domestication theories, Mellen does not believe "one has to assume that the entire stock of domestic cats we have today resulted from one domestication process. Several theories [about domestication] make sense, and each of those may be true."

Are Cats Really Domesticated?

Charles Darwin suggested that domestication involves more than simply taming an animal. A tame animal, although it is amenable to human handling and attention, is not changed fundamentally by its relationship with people, a relationship that may not extend to that animal's offspring, if it has any.

Domestication entails not only taming animals but also breeding them in captivity and making their reproductive choices for them. Among the effects of domestication

are increased reproductiveness, changes in the animal's temperament, and, in some instances, the atrophy of one or more body organs. Furthermore, domesticated animals are subjugated to the people who have domesticated them.

For their part, however, the majority of cats choose their own mating partners and are more capable than are other domesticated animals of surviving on their own. Thus, as naturalist Claire Necker has written, the cat gains much and yields little in its relationship with humans. This truth is often expressed in the truisms volunteered by people who claim to be "owned" by their cats.

The most pampered house cat, Necker continues, can revert to a state of nature with minimal inconvenience; and the most self-sufficient feral cat is able, when necessary, to accept food and lodging, if not close contact, from humans. Thus, one might ask if the cat is really domesticated; and if so, if it is domesticated to the same degree as are other domesticated animals.

Though the cat has shared living quarters with humans for at least 3,600 years, it is difficult to decide whether cats are the most wild of all the domesticated animals or the most domesticated of all the wild ones. Indeed, a person might argue that the domestic cat is not truly domesticated because humans have exercised little control over its love life—save for the occasional bucket of water tossed from a bedroom window in the middle of a howling night. Owned cats that reproduce usually do so not as a consequence of human intervention but as a result of human disregard for the necessity of having a pet cat neutered or spayed. If the conservative standard of domestication is applied— one in which natural selection has no place—then the cat has been domesticated for little more than one hundred years, the length of time that people have been breeding pedigreed cats. According to this view, pedigreed felines—especially the ones that have been bred in captivity the longest—are the only truly domesticated varieties because their breeding is for the most part rigidly controlled.

Effects of Domestication on Feline Personality

The circumstances attending the cat's domestication help to explain the differences between cats' behavior and that of other domesticated animals, especially dogs. Unlike dogs—which were bred in the pursuit of a wide range of skills and temperament for centuries before they were bred for type and conformation alone—cats have virtually never been bred on purpose, and the ones that have, have been bred mainly for their physical traits. Perhaps that is why, says cat artist Wendy Christensen, "no dog will ever tell you to go away, but occasionally a cat will. Cats don't want to be bothered all the time, and when they want to be left alone, they'll give you their buzz-off expression."

Christensen believes that "cats are more like companions than housemates. I have trouble thinking of cats as pets at all because they are not in any way subservient to you. My calico has never sat in my lap in the ten years she's owned me. She's determined not to be a lap cat. She's very affectionate in her own way, but she will not sit in my lap." But a Burmese cat that Christensen once looked after for a friend who was on vacation was sitting on Christensen's shoulder not long after she and the cat had been introduced.

An American Shorthair breeder reports other significant differences between pedigreed cats and the rest of the feline population. This woman once took a barn cat into her house and bred it to one of her pedigreed males (a type of union sometimes permitted by certain cat-registering groups). When that female had kittens, she would not use the litter pan in the same room where she was raising her youngsters. Unlike the woman's pedigreed females, the barn cat preferred to eliminate away from the nest. Moreover, she was not comfortable about letting her owner handle her kittens, as females who have descended from generations of indoor cats normally will do.

There is something irresistible about an open book, and cats think it is their duty to nest on the pages as though to keep the words and their meanings from wandering away.

The Cat's Shifting Fortunes

Throughout history our relationship with cats has ever been a curious one, writes cat behaviorist Bonnie Beaver, DVM. The consistently inconsistent treatment of cats, more variable than that accorded any other domestic animal, has shaped the modern cat's behavior.

Not long after they had been domesticated, cats were accorded cult status in Egypt. Law forbade "the sinful slaying of a cat," and for "such an evil accident," wrote Diodorus of Sicily, "a Roman citizen was torn to pieces by the infuriated populace of Thebes." Herodotus, the father of history, observed in the fifth century B.C. that when Egyptians' houses caught fire, they were more anxious about their cats than about their possessions. Upon dying, Egyptian cats were mourned, mummified, and buried in a consecrated place.

For all its popularity along the Nile, the cat left few historical footprints once it left Egypt. "There is no proof that [the cat] was domesticated in Babylon or Assyria," wrote Agnes Repplier in *The Fireside Sphinx,* "and what scanty information we can gather as the centuries roll on is of a dishearteningly fabulous character. As a plaything, as a pretty household toy, [the cat] was carried from Africa to Europe a few hundred years before the Christian era." In India "the house cat was known from a very early period," about the time of Christ, and "her first entrance into the Chinese Empire appears to have been around 400 A.D."

Other observers place the cat in China at least fifteen hundred years earlier. In any case, the Chinese attitude toward cats was somewhat inscrutable. Cats were suspected of bringing poverty into a house, and the only antidote against this affliction was, ironically, a ceramic figure of a cat gazing into the distance. The Chinese also believed that the older and uglier the cat, the greater the fortune that would befall its owner.

"The saddest gap in the chronicles of the cat," said Repplier, was "her conspicuous absence from 'the glory that was Greece,' from 'the grandeur that was Rome'—an absence which extended over many hundreds of years." This absence was caused in part, no doubt, by the firm of Weasel, Marten, and Polecat, which held a near monopoly on the vermin-chasing concessions in Greece and Rome.

No matter how they behaved when at home, the Romans did introduce the domestic cat to all parts of their empire, including England. They also brought the cat to central Europe.

Because Mohammed's favorite animal was the cat, it has always enjoyed favor in Islamic countries. But Christianity's treatment of cats

In this frontispiece of a seventeenth-century book, a witch names her familiars—the supernatural spirits, often in the form of animals, that attend certain persons or demons.

frequently has been unchristian. When cats were introduced into Europe, they were believed to have protected the Christ child from the Devil's mouse. In a few places, laws were passed to protect cats. In 936, Howel Dda, a prince in southern central Wales, issued a law safeguarding domestic cats.

As time passed, however, the independent nature of cats and their prominent eyes led people to associate cats with Diana, the moon goddess. Legend, as we have noted, says that Diana created the cat to mock the sun god Apollo. This association of cats with the moon eventually led to the association of cats with witchcraft, and that eventually led to the heinous mistreatment of cats.

The cat's descent into disfavor and abuse began toward the middle of the thirteenth century. The Christian church—an institution never fond of cats despite their usefulness in combating the plague-bearing rats that frequently hitched a ride to Europe on the ships of Crusaders returning from the Holy Land—had always been suspicious of cats because they allegedly were not mentioned in the Bible. When a pagan fertility cult, using cats in its rites and pledging allegiance to Freyia, the Norse goddess of love and fertility, sprang up in the Rhineland, the Church blew its miters, reacting as if bowl-headed, medieval precursors of rap singers who advocate the killing of policemen had just come to town.

For the next four hundred and fifty years it was open season on cats throughout Europe. Cats were believed to be the familiars of witches or, worse yet, witches in cats' clothing. In the fifteenth century, Pope Innocent VIII encouraged the destruction of cats as part of a program designed to protect the interests of the Catholic church by eliminating the practice of witchcraft. Whereas centuries ago it had been a crime to bring harm to a cat, it was now an offense to give shelter to one.

Medieval cats suffered especially during Lent, notes Zeuner. Their persecution began on the first Sunday in Lent when cats in the Ardennes were thrown into bonfires or roasted on the ends of long poles or in wicker baskets. Cats also were sacrificed and then buried in Oldenburg, Westphalia, Belgium, Switzerland, and Bohemia. They were burnt on Shrove Tuesday in the Vosges, and at Easter in Alsace.

As the cat's popularity began to revive in the seventeenth century, people made room in their lives and holes in their doors for cats.

The sustained malice toward cats, horrific though its scope, eventually turned to renewed acceptance. One suspects that cats' skill in catching rodents, a skill that had led originally to the cat's domestication, was instrumental in refurbishing its reputation. Plagues started by the disease-carrying fleas to which rats are hosts descended upon Europe and England recurringly from 1347, when the Black Death devastated Europe, until 1665, when the Great Plague of London killed 68,596 people between July and October. These troubles, one surmises, eventually led people to a reacceptance of the cat, the best rat-control device then known to humankind.

Moreover, at the close of the sixteenth century, civilization began to break out in western Europe. "Life grew softer, sweeter, replete with self-indulgence and self-satisfaction," wrote Repplier. "All things

were working harmoniously for the reestablishment of the cat in popular esteem."

The first signs of the cat's restoration appeared in France. The doors of French country houses built between the middle of the sixteenth and the seventeenth centuries were furnished with cutouts that allowed cats to come and go as they pleased. Eventually, people in other western European countries began making entranceways in their lives, if not in their portals, for their cats.

The cat's restoration was accelerated in the eighteenth century when the brown rat invaded Europe, writes Michael W. Fox, PhD, DSc, in *Understanding Your Cat.* Because cats were humankind's only ally in the war against the invader, people developed a new respect for cats, which began to appear as sentries in post offices, warehouses, stores, barracks, and anyplace else where they might be expected to help contain or reduce the rat population.

The cat's standing was further restored, writes Fernand Mery, a French veterinarian, in *The Life, History and Magic of the Cat,* when Louis Pasteur, in the nineteenth century, identified microbes as the cause of many diseases. Because microbes were associated with dirt, zoophobia (the fear of animals) caused many people to shun anything with four legs, especially if the four-legged creature possessed an odor.

Cats, which take pains to keep themselves clean and sweet smelling, were the only animals most people considered safe to keep in the house. Thus, says Fox, people began to appreciate the cat's virtues, a development for which cats are indebted to the brown rat and to Louis Pasteur.

The cat's fortunes in America reflected its fortunes in Europe. The Pilgrims brought cats to America in the seventeenth century, most likely because cats served as the principal method of rodent control on British vessels bound for the New World. Along with the cat, however, came the witchcraft cult, and soon there were witchcraft trials in this country also. In time, two thousand accusations of witchcraft would be upheld in colonial courts.

The Cat's Status Today

Cats are held in higher esteem in the United States today than at any other time in this country's history. Indeed, the esteem in which cats are held approaches, in some instances, the deference they enjoyed in ancient Egypt. During the 1980s the cat population of the United States grew faster than kudzu. According to the Pet Food Institute, the feline congregation in this country increased by more than one third during the last decade—at the end of which there were 57.9

million cats presiding over 27.7 million households—and sometime in 1985 cats overtook dogs as the most plentiful companion animals in the land. (Dogs, however, remain more popular. A greater percentage of households own dogs—36.5 percent—than own cats, 30.9 percent.)

Cats' chief practical value these days lies in supporting a wooly mammoth's share of commerce. Cats consume nearly 3 billion pounds of food, retail, for which their owners spend more than $2.5 billion. In addition, cat owners spend roughly $2 billion on veterinary care annually and millions more on combs, shampoos, flea collars, brushes, kitty litter, toys, vitamins, and just about anything else you could think of—from spray cologne at $1.25 the ounce in scents reminiscent of Chanel, Giorgio, Opium, Obsession, or Aramis to leopard-patterned stud pants for male cats who produce their own spray cologne.

Cats fit our safe-sex, two-careers, deferred-child-raising, one-person-household times as snugly as the dust cover on a BMW or a dead bolt. Unlike dogs, whose needs expand to fill all the available room in your life, cats remain user-friendly on a modest amount of program space. You do not have to walk your cat at 5:00 A.M. in a nor'easter or turn down a sudden invitation to go sailing off the Florida Keys because it isn't safe to leave the cat alone in the house

overnight. What's more, cats occasion lower medical fees than do dogs. Small wonder, then, that these small wonders in fur appear on so many T-shirts, coffee mugs, tote bags, Christmas cards, book covers, calendars, automobile windows, and sofas in late twentieth-century America.

Yet despite their present lionization, cats also appear in shelters with woeful regularity. According to the American Humane Association's *Animal Shelter Reporting Study 1990,* between 5.7 and 9.5 million cats (or four out of every five cats brought into animal shelters in the United States) were euthanized that year. The number of cats euthanized annually had dropped 43 percent between 1985 and 1988, but by 1990 that number had increased 33 percent. Ironically, Americans are putting cats to death, albeit humanely, in much greater numbers than during the Middle Ages when cats were being persecuted outright.

Animal-shelter personnel have been preaching the spay-and-neuter gospel for years, but although education and outreach have their purposes, they also have their limitations. Therefore, some members of the animal-welfare community have turned to legislation in an effort to insure compliance when it cannot be inspired. In a dramatic and controversial move, the Humane Society of the United States recently challenged breeders of pedigreed dogs and cats, who produce nearly 3 million puppies and kittens annually, to observe a voluntary, one-year moratorium on breeding in order to help reduce the surplus-animal population.

Legislation now is considered a fundamental part of the campaign to eliminate pet overpopulation. Such legislation may require (with a few considered exceptions) that persons may not keep more than a specified number of animals without a license to do so, that all animals above a certain age be neutered or spayed, that all animals be licensed, that the cost of licenses for unaltered animals be significantly higher than the cost of licenses for altered animals, that animals be under their owners' supervision when they are off their owners' property, that persons who breed animals obtain a special license and observe reasonable standards of care for their animals, and, where circumstances warrant, that breeding moratoria be enforced for specified periods of time to achieve specified ends.

Yet whenever such legislation is proposed, special-interest groups materialize to fight that legislation. For the most part these groups comprise dog breeders, cat breeders, the lobbyists from the American Kennel Club and the Cat Fanciers' Association who represent them, and, somewhat surprisingly, a few members of the veterinary and animal-care communities.

Persons who oppose pet-limitation or breeding-control ordinances argue that such ordinances are an abridgement of civil rights, that pedigreed animals rarely wind up in shelters, and that people who support such legislation are wild-eyed, animal-rights radicals who want to phase out or, worse yet, to confiscate all companion animals, breeding and nonbreeding alike.

In truth, no one wants to confiscate companion animals—and keeping animals is a privilege, not a right. What's more, pedigreed animals—as many as 70,000 cats and 660,000 dogs a year—do wind up in shelters, and everyone who produces kittens or puppies con-

This is the face of cat overpopulation: a face on which the perils of a free-roaming existence are etched in scars.

tributes to the surplus-animal population because pedigreed kittens and puppies frequently are purchased by people who might have adopted a homeless youngster from a shelter instead.

The rhetoric of special-interest groups notwithstanding, the millions and millions of unwanted animals consigned to a brutally short existence in the wild or to death in an animal shelter each year argue poignantly for legislation that will improve their condition. For many unwanted cats in this country, living conditions are scarcely better than they were for other cats in the Middle Ages.

Chapter 3

The Better Mousetrap: Design and Function of the Cat

Unlike dogs, which occur in a multitude of sizes and designs, cats are limited in composition. The difference between the largest breed of cat, the Ragdoll, and the smallest breed, the Singapura, is little more than a dozen pounds and less than one square foot at the extreme; and the difference between the longest and the shortest facial profiles among pedigreed cats—namely, between the Siamese and the Persian—is a matter of inches.

Virtually all the disparities between cat breeds, indeed, most cat breeds themselves, do not exist because Nature has decreed they should. Most breeds and the differences among them were fashioned and preserved by cat fanciers along lines of which nature would not always approve.

For its part, the domestic cat, which has been spared manipulation by humans, is a remarkably homogeneous creature. Predominantly shorthaired and often tiger-

Cats have facial scent glands which they use like calling cards to leave an impression with their friends.

striped, the domestic cat measures between 12 and 15 inches (30.5–38.1 cm) from its shoulders to the base of its tail and generally weighs between seven and ten pounds (3.2–4.5 kg).

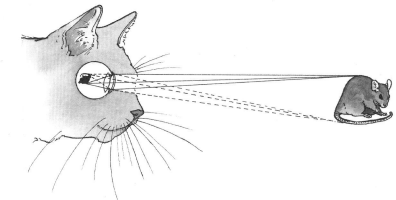

The cat's are a hunter's eyes, set well to the fore and aimed straight ahead to provide the most acute three dimensional picture.

The domestic cat's skeleton is confusingly similar to that of the wild cat from which it is descended. The foremost distinguishing features of the domestic cat are a shorter coat, a smaller brain, a slightly broader skull, a steep rise in the premaxillary bones of the upper jaw, and a longer gap between the canine teeth and the premolars of the lower jaw, which gap is occasioned by the smaller-sized teeth of the domestic cat.

Senses: Sight, Hearing, Taste, Smell, and Touch

Sight

The cat's eye is a gem that reflects a mysterious luster. Pillowed in cushions of fat, the eye is protected by a pair of eyelids that are almost camouflaged by fur. The eyelids close reflexively if anything touches the cat's eyelashes, whiskers, or eyes. (Cats also pos-

sess a third eyelid known as the nictitating membrane or haw. This thin fold of skin, located underneath the eyelid, flicks diagonally upward across the eye, helping to lubricate the cornea. The haw also rises when cats are unwell.)

Most of the cat's eye is surrounded by a dense, white, fibrous membrane called the sclera. The transparent portion of the sclera covering the iris and pupil is known as the cornea. The pupil is the expanding and contracting opening in the iris, which is a contractile, circular diaphragm that forms the colored portion of the eye. Just behind the iris and pupil is the lens, which is suspended by muscles and ligaments. The chamber behind the lens is filled with a jellylike substance called the vitreous humor.

At the rear of the eye chamber is the retina with its blood vessels and light-sensitive rods and cones. Part of the retina is backed by the light-reflecting tapetum lucidum, and part is backed by the dark tapetum nigrum. The optic nerve, made of sensory fibers, transmits signals from the retina to the brain. The short focal length of the eye—a product of the curvature of the cornea and the lens and of the shortness of the cat's eyeball as well—gives the cat a wide-angle-camera view of the world compared to the more narrow view afforded by the human eye.

Cats are born blind. Their eyes remain closed from seven to ten days on average. The retina is not developed completely at first, and a kitten's vision is poor. It improves gradually for about three months, at which time the kitten can see as well as can an adult cat.

The cat's eyes are a hunter's eyes, roughly ¾ to ⅞ inch (1.9–2.2 cm) in diameter, set well to the fore, and aimed straight ahead to provide the most acute three-dimensional picture. The ligaments surrounding the lens of the eye allow the lens to bulge forward, in order to focus on objects close at hand, or to flatten out, in order to focus on objects farther away. Nonetheless, cats are somewhat farsighted. They cannot focus well on any object closer than 30 inches (76 cm) away, and their depth of field is in sharpest focus between 7 and 20 feet (2.1–6.1 m).

Light stimulates a chemical reaction in millions of special cells in the retina, setting off impulses in the optic nerve fibers. The pattern formed by these electrical signals creates images on the retina. These are transmitted via the optic nerve to the visual area of the brain, where they reach the cat's consciousness.

Cats can see moving objects better than stationary ones because specific cells in the cat's brain respond to movement. Thus, cats freeze when they are hunting so that their prey will not notice them.

Although they cannot see in total darkness, cats are most efficient gleaners of light. Their lenses and corneas are larger, relative to the other components of their eyes, than is usual in other species. Moreover, the setting of their lenses—farther back in a cat's than in a human's eyeball—helps to project onto the retina of the cat's eye an image that is five times brighter than the image projected onto a human retina. Cats are able to see in light at least six times more dim than the light in which humans can see.

Cats adjust to varying degrees of light by narrowing or dilating their pupils. In brightest sunlight, the cat's pupils are closed completely except for two tiny openings at the top and bottom of the pupil. In dim light the pupil may be as much as ½ inch (1.3 cm) wide.

At night cats' eyes glitter with an unearthly glow, a reflection of the light striking the mirrorlike tapetum lucidum, which lines most of the surface of the back of the retina. The color reflected by the tapetum lucidum varies with the color of the cat's eye. Yellow- or orange-eyed cats reflect a greenish glow; blue-eyed cats a reddish gleam.

Cats are not colorblind. They can distinguish red from blue and both these colors from white. Yet researchers believe that to the cat, green, yellow, and white are all a whiter shade of pale.

Hearing

The cat's auditory world includes rustlings and reverberations that are more faint and high-pitched than the sounds humans can hear. Because the upper limit of a cat's hearing range is one and a half octaves higher than is a human's, cats can detect the ultrasonic calls of rodents. Humans—thankfully, one supposes—cannot. (The upper limit of a cat's hearing range is higher also than a dog's, although dogs and humans can detect lower sounds than do cats.)

A cat's pinna, or ear flap, is equipped with more than a dozen muscles that allow a cat to rotate it through 180 degrees in order to pinpoint the origin of a sound.

A cat's power of auditory discrimination is not so great as a human's. From a distance of 3 feet (.9 m), two different sources of sound must be at least 3 inches (8 cm) apart before cats can discriminate between them. From the same distance, humans are able to discriminate between two sounds that are only ⅓ inch (.8 cm) apart. Cats, however, are able to ignore the sound of their owners' voices from virtually any distance.

The pinna, or ear flap, is equipped with more than a dozen muscles that confer upon it great mobility. A cat can rotate its pinnae through 180 degrees and can incline them toward the source of a sound. The pinnae gather sound waves and funnel them down through the external auditory canal to the ear drum.

In addition to gathering sound so that a cat can interpret a message, the pinnae enable a cat to send messages, too. There is no mistaking, for example, the message intended by a cat when its ears are drawn back.

Not every component of a cat's ear is devoted to the gathering, transcription, and translation of sound waves. The vestibular apparatus, located in the inner ear, monitors the cat's balance and alignment. Composed of three fluid-filled, semicircular canals and two larger chambers, all of which are filled with millions of tiny hairs, the vestibular apparatus relays information regarding the cat's movement and orientation in space to the brain. In no small part responsible for the cat's vaunted sense of balance, the vestibular apparatus sends signals to the brain whenever the hairs in its chambers move.

In the utricle and saccule, the large chambers of the vestibular apparatus, tiny crystals of calcium carbonate (chalk) press down on the hairs at the bottom of the chambers to relay information to the brain regarding the cat's vertical orientation. In the three semicircular canals, the hairs project into flaps of tissue. Whenever the cat moves its head, the fluid in the semicircular canals sloshes about, moving the hairs in the canals and relaying information to the brain. Because the three semicircular canals are arranged at right angles to one another, they can signal the direction and acceleration of movement.

Taste

The cat's tongue, a pink, flexible rasp, is dotted with tiny, prickly knobs called papillae. The filiform papillae in the center of the tongue are backward-facing hooks, which the cat uses to hold food, to scrape bones clean, or to polish its fur. The fungiform or mushroom-shaped papillae along the front and side edges of the tongue contain taste buds, as do the four or six large vallate or cup-shaped papillae at the back of the tongue.

Researchers employed by cat-food manufacturers have gotten the

If you begin to socialize your cat when she is young, you always will have her in the palm of your hand.

cat's tongue to reveal much about taste reactions and preferences among felines. Of the four basic taste dimensions in mammals—acid, bitter, salt, and sweet—the latter is nonsignificant to cats, a fact revealed by the absence of conduction fibers for sweet in the glossopharyngeal nerve between the tongue and the cerebrum. Cats are virtually alone among mammals in exhibiting no significant reaction to sweets, a phenomenon that is not surprising in a true carnivore like the cat.

Taste is a close neighbor to smell, and both are chemical senses. A cat unable to smell for whatever reason often refuses to eat. Because of the association between taste and smell, cats sometimes smell with their mouths open, an activity known as "flehming." A cat in full flehmen traps airborne molecules of scent on its tongue, then presses the tongue against the opening of its vomeronasal or Jacobson's organ, a ½-inch (1.3 cm), cigar-shaped sac located in the roof of the cat's mouth. A narrow tube leads from the vomeronasal organ to a spot just above the cat's front teeth. (Humans have a vestigial, nonfunctioning trace of this organ in their hard palates.) Catnip, a stranger in the house, a female in season in the yard next door, or other interesting scents may trigger the flehmen reaction in cats.

Smell

Like the senses of taste and touch, the cat's sense of smell has been shown through anatomical evidence to be present at birth. One-day-old kittens have demonstrated an ability to distinguish between salted and nonsalted liquids. Indeed, throughout their lives cats are greatly sensitive to the taste of water. They, more so than humans, one suspects, can tell the difference between Evian, Perrier, Poland Spring, and other bottled products. Human perception of such differences is confined mainly to observations regarding price.

Often, when neonatal kittens are moved from a familiar nest, they begin to cry because they are distressed that the smell of the new nest is different from the smell of the old, familiar one. Kittens do not settle in the new nest until their mother rejoins them and reassures them, by her smell, that all is well. (The sense of smell is thought to be responsible, too, for a kitten's inclination to return to the same nipple each time it nurses.)

In a real sense cats read with their noses, sniffing studiously all new objects, persons, other ani-

mals, and food they encounter. But there's more to the sense of smell than meets the nose. Behind the cat's nose lies a maze of bones and cavities. When cats breathe, air passing through this maze is warmed and moistened. Part of the air is channeled across the olfactory mucosa, which covers a relatively large area, 3 to 6 square inches (20–40 square cm), in the cat's nasal lining. This is nearly twice the size of the olfactory mucosa of rabbits, which are comparable in size to the cat, or of humans, which are much larger. The olfactory mucosa contains a complex arrangement of cells. The most important are the 200 million olfactory cells, which are sensitive to volatile airborne substances.

In addition, a cat's sense of smell is supercharged by the subethmoid shelf in the cat's nose. After a cat sniffs at something purposefully, the sniffed air is not expelled when the cat exhales. Instead of moving through the nasal passages, into the lungs, and back out through the nasal passages, sniffed air and the scent molecules it carries remain in the cat's nose above the subethmoid shelf so that the air can be "read" more closely by the cat.

The order of difference between a cat's sense of smell and ours is considerable. We can smell an unpeeled clove of garlic faintly from a close perspective. Yet we smell garlic keenly when it is crackling in olive oil in the skillet. The cat can smell garlic at that high-impact level before we get it out of the shopping bag. Thus, a cat's sense of smell enables it to tell far more about the age, sex, and health of other cats than we humans, with our feeble senses of smell, can imagine.

Touch

The cat's sense of touch conveys sensations of pressure, cold, warmth, and pain. A newborn kitten employs its sense of touch—more specifically its knack for detecting warmth—to find its way to its mother in the nest. This heat-sensing ability continues to develop as the kitten matures. The heat receptors in an adult cat's nose are sensitive enough to detect differences in temperature as small as 0.9°F (0.5°C).

Although warmth and cold receptors are present all over a cat's body, the cat is relatively insensitive to high and low temperatures except on its face and paws. For example, cats do not react to heat at temperatures below 126°F (52°C) on the average, whereas humans feel discomfort when their skin temperature reaches 112°F (44°C).

The most sensitive touch receptors are located in a cat's whiskers and its paws, especially in its forepaws. A cat's whiskers, or vibrissae, contain bundles of nerves that send impulses to the brain along the same channel used by the eyes. Whiskers are sensitive to contact and to movements in the air. If you touch the whiskers over a cat's eyes, the cat will blink. Whiskers also are used to gauge the size of an opening a cat is investigating and to help a cat "see" objects in the dark by detecting the slight eddies that these objects create in the air around them.

The importance of a cat's forepaws as a source of tactile information is suggested by the size of the area of the cat's brain that receives messages from the forepaws. In fact, all four of the cat's paw pads are extremely sensitive. They provide information about the texture of objects and about their temperature as well. Some people believe that a cat's paw pads can detect vibrations, which would explain why some cats appear to be able to "hear" through

From the time they are born, kittens use their ability to detect warmth to find their way to their mother in the nest. This heat-sensing ability continues to develop, and adult cats are able to detect differences in temperature as small as 0.9° F (0.5° C).

their feet. (If a person were to crawl across the floor or back yard, the sensations recorded by the hands would be somewhat similar to those recorded by a cat's paws.)

Besides transmitting painful impulses to the brain, the cat's sense of touch conveys pleasurable sensations, too. A mother washes her kittens with her sandpapery tongue and moves them toward her in the nest with her paws. From this, kittens learn to associate certain kinds of touches with a caring attitude. Later in life adult cats make the same association upon receiving attentive—or even absent-minded—stroking from a human hand, which recreates the pleasure a cat felt when it was licked by its mother in the nest.

Petting and grooming are said to reduce tension by slowing down a cat's heart rate. Perhaps this is why a cat often will start to wash itself in situations that evoke doubt or stress.

Paradoxically, some cats will strike at the hand that pets them. This is a curious, disconcerting, and somewhat puzzling response to what presumably has been enjoyable contact. Feral cats that react this way to being petted can be excused on the grounds that they are not used to such affection or have not developed enough trust in people, but one is hard put to imagine why some domesticated cats react this way occasionally, too. Perhaps in the cat's mind there can be too much of a good thing.

The sense of touch is employed also when a cat chooses a place to sleep. Cats like warm, soft fabrics and often will refuse to stay on the lap of someone wearing a cold or slippery dress or trousers or clothing made of synthetic fiber. Not surprisingly, cats always seek out warm sleeping spots (the crooks of human knees are a favorite site). As their faces are the most cold-sensitive parts of their bodies, cats are quick to curl up into a ball when they are cold, using their tails as mufflers for keeping their faces warm.

Muscles

Striped (voluntary) The cat's skeleton is decorated in wreaths of voluntary muscles, more than five-hundred weight-pulling garlands of muscle in all. Voluntary muscles, so called because they operate under the brain's conscious command, often are called skeletal muscles because their chief function is to move the cat's skeleton, and hence the cat, from place to place. They also are called striped or striated muscles because their appearance is characterized by latitudinal stripes.

Each skeletal muscle comprises numerous bundles of long, cylindrical cells known as fibers. These fibers, from 1 to 40 millimeters long and from 10 to 100 micrometers wide, are about the size of a human hair.

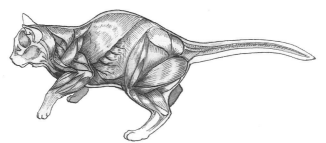

The cat has more than five hundred skeletal muscles. Each muscle comprises numerous bundles of long, cylindrical cells known as fibers, which are roughly the size of a human hair.

Skeletal muscles receive electrical impulses from the brain after it has processed information provided by the senses. The motor cortex, which commands movement, and the cerebellum, which coordinates balance, are the shop stewards in the brain that issue work orders for the cat's skeletal muscles.

Depending on the kind of action it wants to initiate, the brain will send either of two electrical messages to the motor-end nerve attached to each unit of skeletal muscle fiber. Tonic stimulation (or low electrical frequency in long bursts) governs on-going activity such as paw washing. Phasic stimulation (or high electrical frequencies in short bursts) activates muscle fibers when sudden action, such as racing across the living room in pursuit of a thrown toy, is required.

Muscles display a full-speed-ahead, all-or-nothing approach to life. Thus, the power of a contraction is governed by the number of muscle fibers that are ordered to contract, not by the extent to which they are ordered to contract. If the brain estimates that only two-thirds of a muscle's power is needed to perform some action, only two-thirds of that muscle's fibers will receive the call to arms.

From the first time a kitten paddles toward its mother, it seeks to command its skeletal muscles. These soon will enable the kitten to scrimmage with its littermates for a place in the food line, to knead contentedly against its mother's belly, to crawl, wobble, stand, totter, fall, right itself, ratchet its head about uncertainly, fall, rise again, and, finally, walk. Secured to the skeleton by tendons, skeletal muscles always are arranged in pairs—antagonists and protagonists that work in cooperative opposition to each other.

When a cat jumps, for example, it crouches on its heels by contracting two muscles: the hamstring, a flexor muscle located behind the thigh bone, and the tibialis, a flexor muscle located in front of the tibia and fibula bones. At that point the corresponding extensor muscles that were stretched while the hamstring and tibialis were contracting, contract powerfully themselves, hurling the cat temporarily beyond gravity's dominion.

Smooth (involuntary) Both chapters of the United Muscular Workers Union—voluntary and involuntary—begin to form about 11 or 12 days after fertilization when a kitten embryo is but a hopeful confederation of cells scarcely ⅛ inch (4 mm) long. Involuntary (or smooth) muscles, which are not consciously controlled by the cat, are found in working-class locations such as the alimentary canal and the inner spaces of the urogenital and respiratory systems of the cat. Smooth muscles are also on the job in the walls of the arterioles, helping to determine arteriole size and, thereby, to maintain blood pressure.

Whereas skeletal muscles occur most often in bundles, smooth muscle fibers are arranged usually in sheets, small groups, or—especially in the dermis—singly. And even though smooth muscle fibers lie parallel to one another, they are not arranged in the lock-step, close-order drill of the skeletal muscles. The tip of one smooth muscle fiber, for example, often will be found cheek by jowl with the midsection of another fiber in the same sheet. That is why smooth muscles do not exhibit latitudinal stripes as do skeletal muscles.

Not only are they imprecise in their orientation, smooth muscle fibers also are smaller than are skeletal muscle fibers. The latter range from 1 to 40 millimeters in length and from 10 to 100 micrometers in width. Smooth muscles generally are .2 millimeters long and 6 micrometers wide. Understandably, the contractions made by smooth muscles are not so large as are the contractions made by skeletal muscles.

Like the guitar and bass in a jazz combo, smooth and skeletal muscles play their parts in the body's harmonious composition. The smooth muscles keep the beat, marking time like a metronome, while the skeletal muscles play improvisations on the melody, lending grace, style, and majesty to the movements of the cat.

Skeleton

Officially classified as connective tissue designed to bear weight, bone lends definition and support to the cat's body and protection to its internal organs. There are 244 bones in the feline skeleton—from the stately, immobile sections of the neurocranium to the nimble, trinket-like phalanges in the toes.

Cartilage, bone's pearl-handled ally in the skeletal system, performs several important functions as well. It coats the ends of bones in movable joints, allowing them to rub against each other with minimal friction and wear. Cartilage also connects the ribs to the sternum, forming a safety deposit box for the heart and lungs. Without cartilage a cat's ribs would sink like soup bones in a stock pot. What's more, cartilage supports the epiglottis, larynx, trachea, bronchi, and external ear.

The skeletal system begins developing in the kitten embryo before a female gives any signs that she is pregnant. About 11 days after fertilization has occurred, the embryo, a scant 1/5 inch (4 mm) long, starts to attach itself to the uterine wall. At the same time cells begin to matriculate to one of three concentric layers forming in the embryo—ectoderm, mesoderm, or endoderm. Through this process, known as differentiation, cells become structurally and functionally unique.

When differentiated cells continue to multiply after reaching their destinations in the embryo, they do so in kind, but they are still subject to further modification by genetic mandate. Some of the cells in the mesoderm, for example, develop into mesenchymal cells; and these, in turn, develop into chondroblasts, which give rise to cartilage, or into osteoblasts, which give rise to bone.

As chondroblasts reproduce, they build a cartilaginous model of the skeleton which will someday inhabit the mature cat. By and large, the majority of bone in the adult skeleton will be formed within and upon this slight, delicate precursor. One day the skeleton will collaborate with muscle to transform the cat into a statement of power and grace (or klutzy charm); but in the young embryo, the skeleton—so decisive in its prime—is a pliant approximation of its future self.

Bone can be cataloged into three classes according to shape: long, flat, and irregular. The radius and ulna in the front legs, as well as the tibia and fibula in the hind legs are long bones. The scapula or shoulder blade is a flat bone. So are the bones of the skull and face. The metatarsals and metacarpals in the feet are irregular bones.

Cats reach skeletal maturity sometime between eight months and one year of age. At that point, what you see is what you are going to see. Growth plates—the cartilaginous layers situated between the shafts and the ends of bones—do not normally close until a cat is one year old. Sometimes growth plates remain open longer. If they do, there is potential for growth, but significant bone growth beyond the first year of a cat's life is as rare as the kid who grows six inches between high school and college.

Part protein, part mineral, mostly water, the skeletal system of the cat is a bona fide marvel. Practically maintenance free, it is almost injury free, too, since automobiles, the major source of broken bones in cats, seldom venture indoors. (And bone, once broken, even exhibits a good-natured inclination to effect its own repair within reasonable limits.) In addition, bone disease, like bone injury, is an infrequent problem with cats, who are less prone than are some companion animals to osteoarthritis, rheumatoid arthritis, and the other infirmities that come with the dismal territory of old age. Indeed, like the finest of silent partners, bone makes its presence felt in the cat without being seen or heard.

Intelligence

Although writers from Plutarch in the first century to Montaigne in the sixteenth had remarked on the cleverness of animals, the subject of animal intelligence was declared so much hogwash by Rene Descartes, the father of modern philosophy, in the mid-seventeenth century. From then until the publication of Charles Darwin's *On the*

This Chartreux begs to differ with its countryman René Descartes (1596–1650), who believed that all animals were merely "beast machines."

Origin of Species in 1859, animals were considered "beast machines": dumb, hidebound creatures of habit and heredity that reacted to their surroundings, but never reflected on them, much less on themselves.

On the Origin of Species, which sold out the day it was published, rattled the cages of the scientific establishment; and for the half century following the Darwinian revolution, psychologists and biologists were eager to study the mental experiences—and by extension, the intelligence—of animals. Nevertheless, investigators still were inclined to put Descartes before their horse sense. This helped open the door to behaviorism, which closed the door, around 1920, on any suggestions that animals—and people, too, according to many behaviorists—are mentally capable of anything more sophisticated than reacting to external stimuli.

Though pre-Darwinian attitudes regarding animal intelligence unfortunately inform much of the populace today, roughly 25 years ago scientists began to ask whether human beings alone—among all the earth's inhabitants—possess the capacities for thought and self-consciousness. And if so, what is the proof for these unique, human capabilities? And wherein lies their source? If not, what evidence is there that other creatures can think? And which nonhumans are the most intelligent thinkers?

Manifestations of intelligence abound in the animal kingdom. One example comes from Marine World. To enlist the cooperation of captive dolphins in removing litter that had blown into their pool, trainer Jim Mullen devised a trash-for-fish plan whereby dolphins were paid according to scale for every scrap of refuse they retrieved. The system worked swimmingly, but Mullen noticed that one dolphin, Mr. Spock, soon had a virtual monopoly on trash hauling. Curious about Spock's success, Mullen watched through an underwater observation window while an assistant directed a pool-cleaning session. Thus did Mullen learn that the enterprising Spock was hoarding paper bags full of trash beneath a platform and was cashing them in at feeding time.

Another manifestation of thought among animals was provided by a young baboon. One day this youngster observed an adult female baboon digging roots from the cracked, dry earth. He looked around after a moment and, seeing no other animals in sight, screamed bloody murder as though he had been attacked. His mother came running, saw the alleged offending female, over which she held dominance, and swiftly uprooted her. The sly, mendacious male then helped himself to a free lunch.

Were either of these behaviors exhibited by a young child, psychologists would consider them manifestations of the child's developing intelligence; but since the agents in question were not human, most members of the scientific community for most of this and preceding centuries would have explained these actions in terms of conditioning, stimulus-response theory, hereditary instinct, or some other mechanistic paradigm. The dolphin and the baboon—like the dog that waxes euphoric at the sight of a lead or the cat that zooms toward the kitchen like a heat-seeking missile at the sound of a can being opened—are given an A for promptness of response, but no credit for anything more. To suggest otherwise in scientific company—or even to raise certain questions—has been to risk being regarded with the condescension and amusement usually accorded someone who shows up at a black-tie dinner in a Hawaiian shirt.

Fortunately, some scientists have begun to rethink the notion of animal intelligence. Their conclusions were summed up nicely in 1987 in *New Scientist* magazine. "It is highly improbable that [animal] brains anatomically and physiologically so much more similar than dissimilar to our own don't generate a broadly comparable pattern of consciousness. No appreciation of poetry, perhaps. Not much feel for the works of the Impressionists, maybe. Little in the way of mathematical skills, I dare swear. Small thought for the prospects of eternal salvation or damnation, I'll warrant.

But no fear, no pleasure, no frustration, no anticipation of habitual delights or apprehension of unpleasant happenings or disappointments? Rubbish!"

And no thinking? Rubbish again.

People who believe that animals possess intelligence often believe that one species possesses more than another. The cat, which has a one- to two-ounce brain with perhaps 10 billion neurons, has been ranked somewhere between a gerbil and a marmoset on a cerebral-development chart. But, warns Daniel Q. Estep, PhD, a certified animal behaviorist who practices in Littleton, Colorado, "it's difficult to compare intelligence across species. Each species is born with a predisposition to learn certain things or to develop certain kinds of learning abilities that have been favored in their evolutionary path.

"Dogs are easy to train because they're highly social, and the ability to respond to social reinforcement is so important to dogs living in a pack in the wild that its development has been favored in their history. But cats in the wild are essentially solitary or at best colonial animals. They don't have a complex social organization, nor do they hunt in packs. Therefore, some kinds of learning are not important to cats, so they don't learn in the same sorts of ways that dogs do.

"Oftentimes people assume that cats are stupid because they don't learn some tasks as quickly as a dog learns them. But I could devise a series of tests for which cats would always come out on top, and I could probably design another series of tests in which dogs would always come out on top.

"People often want to compare cats to dogs. They'll say, 'Nobody ever trained a cat like Lassie.' But I like to point out that there aren't any dogs I know that will use a litter box."

So which is smarter, a cat or a dog?

"In some cases," replies Estep, "all you're really measuring is the intelligence of the tester."

Vocal Communication

Communication includes the exchange of thoughts, feelings,

needs, moods, information, trust, and desires. It involves listening as well as speaking, and where the cat is concerned, it entails listening not only with our ears but with our eyes and speaking not only with our voices but with our gestures, too.

Cats are not as good at expressing their emotions with their faces as are dogs. Cats can move their whiskers and their ears in an impressive variety of ways, but they do not command the facial muscles necessary to produce the full range of expressions—from joy to indignation to a woebegone, hangdog self-pity—with which dogs manipulate their way into their owners' hearts. Thus, cats rely on vocal communication and on body language to reveal what is on their minds.

Some cat breeds, most notably the Siamese and its Oriental brethren, chatter unceasingly. But the domestic cat, for the most part, shows more respect for the sounds of silence. With the exception of females in season, domestic cats save their voices for special occasions: meowing dejectedly if they have been shut into a closet by accident, grousing sharply if you have snagged their fur while grooming them, or sounding the alarm when they want you to get up and fix breakfast. Cats may also—for no apparent reason other than the spontaneous expression of their joy at being alive and in your company—pop into your lap with a jolly *chirrup.* (There are, of course, other vocalizations that cats use when speaking to one another or to birds on the far side of a window.)

No matter what the occasion, when your cat speaks to you, there is a reason. Unlike people, cats seldom talk to admire the sound of their own voices. You should, therefore, respond when your cat speaks. The cat stuck in the closet wants to hear how sorry you are for its misfortune and how you will never let this indignity occur again. The cat whose fur has been ruffled wants a similar apology. The cat waking you up for breakfast would like a cheery "good morning" and some food on its plate. The cat making a joyful noise would appreciate a soft "Hello," an attentive "What is it?" or a fond "You don't say?" By responding to your cat's vocal declarations and entreaties, you build the rapport that is the foundation upon which cat training is based.

A cat's most endearing verbal communication is the silent meow, which has to be seen to be appreciated. A silent meow occurs when a cat opens its mouth and mimes the word *meow* but no sound emerges. Silent meows function as greetings, terms of endearment, all-purpose, unspecified kvetches, and as the feline equivalents of baying at the moon.

Making Sense of Odors

When a cat rubs up against a piece of furniture or a human leg, it leaves a scent mark on that surface. When a cat scratches a tree in the yard or a scratching post or a sofa in the living room, it marks their surfaces, too. Similarly, two cats rubbing heads will leave their scent on one another so they will recognize each other when next they meet. Not surprisingly, your cat will know when you have been to a house where there are other cats, and the cats in that house will have been more than a little interested in you because you came in trailing clouds of scent from your cats at home.

Body Language

Cats are more likely to communicate with their bodies than with their voices. From the tips of their noses to the ends of their tails, cats are like electronic bulletin boards on which a continuous series of messages flows.

Cats can generate at least three of those messages with their tails. Carried erect at a 90-degree angle to the body, the tail broadcasts a message of good cheer and camaraderie. Carried at a less jaunty angle and puffed out in bristling display, the tail is a declaration of war. Twitching slowly from side to side, the tail signals annoyance. The faster the twitch, the greater the itch;

Cats communicate with their bodies as much as they do with their voices. Therefore, to understand a cat's body language, we must learn to listen with our eyes as well as with our ears.

and if twitch turns to lash, beware. Fireworks are about to ensue.

At the other end of the message board, wide-open, attentive eyes signal interest, in a positive fashion, in what a cat sees; whereas a narrow gaze indicates that the cat is not sure if what it sees is interesting or threatening. Cats that gaze at a person and then blink their eyes slowly are sending a message of submission, much as one cat will blink at another by way of de-escalating a face-to-face encounter.

A cat uses its hindquarters to declare affection and trust. This form of communication—in which a cat brushes past the object of its affection and then positions its (the cat's) hindquarters in firsthand proximity to the object's face—may

take the cat-owning novice by surprise, especially if cat and novice are enjoying a nap together. Indeed, most longtime cat owners would prefer that their cats said it with flowers instead.

A more conventional expression of fondness is the full-body flop, a maneuver in which a cat lands first on its side, then rolls onto its back, finally ending up in a semicircle. This fetching invitation to a belly rub is usually inspired by a cat's exuberance at being stroked along its spine or scratched at the base of its tail. Be cautious in accepting this invitation, however, because many cats are ticklish on their bellies. When you reach past their upturned paws to scratch their bellies, you are putting your arm at some risk. Should the cat take a notion to grasp your arm between its front paws and to rabbit-kick your arm with its back paws, you could be in for a bloodletting. Do not panic and try to withdraw your arm suddenly. That will make your situation more perilous because you will be pulling your tender skin against your cat's talonlike claws. Instead of moving your arm backward toward you, move it forward and down through the cat's front legs. Because that is the direction in which your upside-down cat's claws are pointed, you will be disengaging your flesh from their grasp.

Right side up, the cat taps out a variety of messages with its paws. A paw raised softly to a person's cheek or laid gently on the arm is a sign of attachment. A series of taps on the leg or arm is an attempt to bring a person to attention. A smart *whap* with the claws sheathed is a warming that you have violated a cat's sense of propriety. Such warnings often are issued while a cat is being groomed, usually in a spot that is sensitive or ticklish.

Like its tail, a cat's ears convey different messages and emotions. Cats swivel their ears in response to new sounds in the vicinity. They flatten their ears and extend them to the side in response to a frightening stimulus. And they will curl their ears backward in anger.

Cats greet their friends—two-legged and four legged alike—in well-scripted ceremonies. A cat, its tail erect in greeting, will approach a friend and then rub its cheek against the cheek, neck, or face of that friend. This rite not only indicates cordiality, it is a request for permission to enter another individual's air space, and it leaves a trace of the approaching cat's scent on its friend.

A cat's facial muscles may lack the mobility needed to produce a broad range of expressions, but its body is an open book that reveals much about what a cat is thinking and feeling. Arched backs and big tails, for example, are obvious signs of fear and displeasure. A low-slung advance with eyes and tail at half mast is a sign of attack. And a cat that has been reprimanded will frequently sit with its back to its owner to signal its indignation.

Chapter 4

Basic Training for Humans

At the Folies Bérgère in Paris, Agnes Repplier, author of *The Fireside Sphynx,* saw a trained-animal act that included dogs, monkeys, and a cat. The cat "condescended to leap twice through a hoop and to balance herself very prettily on a large rubber ball," wrote Repplier. "She then retired to the top of a ladder, made a deft and modest toilet, and composed herself for slumber. Twice the trainer spoke to her persuasively, but she paid no heed, and evinced no further interest in him nor in his entertainment."

The day after she had observed the cat's performance, Repplier was discussing the show with two friends who had attended the Folies on previous nights. One of her friends said, "The evening I went, the cat did wonderful things; she came down the ladder on her ball, played the fiddle, and stood on her head."

The other friend was incredulous. "The night I went," she said, "the cat did nothing at all except cuff one of the monkeys that annoyed her. She just sat on the ladder and watched the performance. I presumed she was there by way of decoration."

Many household cats make the same presumption. They are quick to decorate a chair near a sunny window but slow to leave it when they are told. They will leap to the top of the stove when they have a mind to but will pay you no mind if you ask them to jump through a

Do not attempt this trick at home until you have established the requisite trust in your cat.

hoop. They will stretch out in the middle of the book you are reading but will walk away scornfully if you ask them to lie down somewhere else. They may have grown accustomed to your face, but they are wont to remind you that they were serenely independent and content before you met. Thus, before you can control your cat, you must try to understand her first.

Why Your Cat Does Not Come When You Call

Of all the signs and wonders to be seen at a dog show, the most wondrous occur in the obedience rings. There dogs of various sizes, shapes, and descriptions heed verbal and visual commands as if they (the dogs) were electronically controlled robots in fur. The handler walks forward; the dog walks obligingly at his or her side. The handler stops; the dog comes to an immediate halt, then sits down promptly to await further instruction. The handler tosses an object; the dog remains seated until he is told to move, then retrieves the object, trots back to the handler, and drops it gently at the handler's feet.

In obedience classes dogs jump, sit, retrieve, lie down, and hold that thought on command. They pick out from a group of objects the one object that a handler has touched,

ignoring the other objects that do not bear the handler's scent. And in one demonstration sure to confound any school teacher who has stepped out of a classroom momentarily only to discover that three felonies have been committed by the time he or she returns, a group of handlers instruct their dogs to lie down, tell them to stay in that position, then leave the ring long enough to have a bite of lunch before they return. When they do, their dogs are sitting precisely where they have been left.

There are no obedience classes at cat shows. And for good reason. Dogs live to please their owners. Cats live to please themselves. Thus, the cat is not the most obedient of creatures. The gentleman who invented cat shows, an English chap named Harrison Weir, was aware of that when he organized the first cat show more than 120 years ago. Weir offered classes for various colors of longhaired cats

Dogs live to please their owners. Cats live to please themselves. That is why there are no obedience classes at cat shows.

and for Royal Cats of Siam. There were classes for hybrids between wild and domestic cats, for gelded cats, for the heaviest cats, and for "Cats Belonging to Working Men"; but there was nary a class for performing cats.

Weir believed that cats have "a natural, sullen antipathy to being taught or restrained or *made* [his emphasis] to do anything to which [their] nature or feelings are averse." High on the cat's list of aversions is coming when its owner calls. A dog may be voice activated, its legs, tail, and tongue springing into action at the sound of its name; but when you call your cat, it may stiffen its legs, swish its tail, or look at you as if you are speaking in tongues, none of which it comprehends.

The only time most cats come when they are called is when they are young kittens in the nest. They respond then to their mother's calls because she provides them with warmth, affection, and food. When it is time to wean her kittens, however, a mother not only stops calling them but also rebuffs their attempts at nursing when they sidle up to her looking for a snack.

No one suggests a causal connection between a kitten's rejection by its mother and an adult cat's unwillingness to come when humans call, but many believe the cat's solitary nature, forged during millions of years of evolution as a solitary hunter, is a logical explanation. Unlike the dog, which in the wild depends on its pack for survival and willingly transfers that dependence to its human pack, the cat need not answer to anyone but itself, for the cat is the consummate freelancer. The only social members of its family are lions and cheetahs. Thus, rather than asking why cats do not come when they are called, we should ask, instead, why should they?

How Cats Learn

Hunting Skills

Kittens learn much by observation, and the first teacher they observe is usually their mother, who not only knows best but also teaches best if laboratory experiments are to be credited. In one series of experiments, kittens that watched their mother press a bar to obtain food learned to imitate her behavior faster than did kittens that watched a strange female cat obtain food in the same manner. Moreover, kittens left to their own trial-and-error

Having learned basic hunting skills from its mother, this kitten is off practicing its footwork on its own.

devices in this situation never made the connection between pressing the bar and obtaining food. In other experiments cats also learned to escape from puzzle boxes and to pull a string to secure food. Finally, cats have proven to be adept at avoidance learning. They are quick to avoid unpleasant experiences (being squirted with a water pistol) and the circumstances (jumping onto the kitchen table) in which those experiences occur.

More interesting than the lessons cats have learned in laboratory experiments is the motivation that inspired their learning. Unlike dogs, cats would not produce the desired behavior if their only reward for doing so was a reunion with the experimenter. Cats expected to be paid for their performances, and the coin of the cat realm is food. The experimenter was not without influence, however. Cats worked more diligently for a reward when the experimenter was the person who fed them each day. (Among kittens, freedom to explore was more inspiring than food as a reward for learning, which proves that cats, like people, are not born materialistic. Life makes them that way.)

Just as kittens in the confines of a laboratory do, kittens raised in the wild learn best from their mothers, who teach by example. When kittens are about five or six weeks old, a mother cat will begin to bring dead prey to the nest and to eat it in front of her kittens. After the kittens' nat-

Like all good teachers, mother cats use visual aids to supplement their lessons.

ural hunting instincts have begun to emerge in response to this stimulus, the mother will bring live (or half live) prey to the nest and release it, intervening only if the prey appears to be in danger of escaping. Eventually she will take the kittens hunting with her. Instead of teaching her kittens to hunt, the mother creates a learning situation that allows the kittens' instincts to develop naturally. (In sociopolitical gibberish this would be called empowering the kittens. It is, perhaps, what our cats are trying to do when they lay mice at our doors, although some romantics believe the mice constitute a present.) Because the kittens' hunting lessons depend on a steady supply of visual aids, mothers that hunt best, teach best; kittens whose mothers are good hunters are most likely to grow up to be good hunters, too; and kittens that are not raised by a member of their own species tend to have hunting deficiencies.

Kittens' reliance on observational learning is so great that they will imitate their mother's choice of food even if that choice is nontraditional. Researchers, to whom such matters seem to be important, have trained adult female cats to eat bananas or mashed potatoes. When those females' kittens were given a choice between meat pellets and either bananas or mashed potatoes, most of the kittens ate the bananas or mashed potatoes.

Litter-box Use

According to conventional wisdom, kittens are taught to use a litter pan by their mothers. Suzanne Hetts, PhD, a certified animal behaviorist on staff at the Denver Dumb Friends League in Colorado, disputes that wisdom. "There are many citations, both scientific and anecdotal, of orphaned kittens using a litter box without ever being shown how to do that by an adult cat," says Hetts. "When kittens start to become more mobile at about four weeks of age, they intuitively begin scratching and playing in soft, loose surfaces. As they mature, in addition to playing in loose surfaces they begin to eliminate in them, and they will do that without ever having observed an adult animal doing it."

Hetts also challenges the notion that the best way to teach an orphaned or a recalcitrant kitten to use a pan is by placing it in the pan, taking hold of its paws, and making scratching motions in the litter. "In my experience," she says, "that has the potential to be a lot more aversive than it is positive or pleasant. You could create litter-box problems by doing it because the kitten might not like being handled that way and will begin to avoid the pan as a result."

Tricks Your Cat May Know Already

Many people who have considered the circumstances surrounding the cat's domestication agree with zoologist Paul Leyhausen, who argued that cats domesticated themselves. Like their self-domesticating ancestors, cats today often learn tricks for which there are no instructors other than the cats themselves.

Your cat may know, for example, that you do not close the bedroom

Performing is a participle not often dangled in front of cat, but as this cat demonstrates, the union is not an all together foreign one.

Opening doors that have not been closed securely is one of several tricks your cat may know already.

door tightly all the time. Hence, if she pushes against it, she may get to enjoy an afternoon nap in the middle of your bed. Your cat probably knows also that if she rubs against your leg when you are in the kitchen late in the afternoon, she will be fed. Experience has taught your cat, perhaps, that it is all right to lie on the kitchen table if you are not in the kitchen. Your cat may know that if she sits by you quietly when you are enjoying a bowl of ice cream before retiring, you will let her lick the bowl when you are finished.

Your cat knows that if she sits by the kitchen door and meows, she is likely to be allowed outside. Your cat may know that if she walks up to you and flops over on her back you will rub her belly. Our 12-year-old cat, who was given a high-calorie vitamin paste each morning, knew to keep a vigil on the bathroom sink, which is where my wife

fed her in order to keep our other cats from interfering in the ceremony. One Birman owner has a cat that puts his paws on his owner's shoulders and licks her hair, not for any specific reward, but because the cat knows, according to his owner, "that if he does that he can have anything he wants."

No doubt all cat owners in America could supply examples of tricks their cats have learned without having had to be taught. If we contemplate those tricks even briefly, we will see that cats, no matter how old they are, still respond best to the stimuli that drew them to their mothers in the nest: warmth, affection, and food—though not necessarily in that order.

Great Expectations: What a Cat Can Learn

In 1889 Harrison Weir wrote an engaging book called *Our Cats and All About Them.* In a chapter devoted to performing cats, Weir quoted a writer who had been to the Royal Aquarium in Westminster to see one of several companies of performing cats that had been appearing in London.

"On each side of the stage there were cat kennels, from which the cats made their appearance on a given signal, ran across, on or over whatever was placed between, and

A cat's sense of balance, which begins to develop when a cat is quite young, is controlled by the vestibular apparatus located in the inner ear.

disappeared quickly into the opposite kennels. But about it all there was a decided air of *timidity,* and an eagerness to *get the performance over,* and *done with it.* [Emphasis, here and below, the original author's.] When the cats came out they were caressed and encouraged, which seems to have a soothing effect, and I have a strong apprehension that they received some dainty morsel when they reached their destination. One ran up a pole at command, over which there was a cap at the top, into which it disappeared for a few seconds, evidently for some reason, food *perhaps.* It then descended. But before this supreme act several cats had crossed a bridge of chairs, stepping only on the backs, until they reached the opposite house or box into which to retire. The process was repeated, and the performance varied by two cats crossing the

bridge together, one passing over and the other under the horizontal rung between the seat and the top of the chair. A long plank was next produced, upon which was placed a row of wine-bottles at intervals; and the cats ran along the plank, winding in and out between the bottles, first to the right, then to the left, without making a mistake. This part of the performance was varied by placing on the top of each bottle a flat disc of thick wood; one of the cats strode then from disc to disc, without displacing or upsetting a bottle, while the other animal repeated its serpentine walk on the plank below. The plank being removed, a number of trestles were brought in, and placed at intervals in a row between the two sets of houses, when the cats, on being called, jumped from trestle to trestle, varying the feat by leaping through a hoop, which was held up by the trainer between the trestles. To this succeeded a performance on the tight rope, which was not the least curious part of the exhibition. A rope being stretched across the arena from house to house, the cats walked across in turn, without making a mistake. Some white rats were then brought and placed at intervals along the rope, when the cats, recrossing from one end to the other, strode over the rats without injuring them. A repetition of this feat was rendered a little more difficult by substituting for rats, which sat pretty quietly in one place, several white mice and small birds, which were more restless, and kept changing their positions. The cats re-crossed the rope and passed over all these obstacles without even noticing the impediments placed in their way, with one or two exceptions, when they stopped and cossetted one or more of the white rats, two of which rode triumphantly on the back of a large black cat."

Similar feats of cat training can be found in reports from eighteenth-century France to twentieth-century America. Indeed, the tricks a cat may learn are limited only by its trainer's imagination, patience, and love of cats. But that is a big "only," especially the last part. If you are on a last-name basis with your cat, you will have a hard time teaching it to come when you call, let alone teaching it to do anything more complex. If you ignore your cat most of the time, chances are she will ignore you when you ask her to do something.

Many cats can be taught to perform at home, but the real troopers are the ones that can take their act on the road.

Lesser Expectations: What Your Cat May Learn

Most people who learn to play the piano never play in public. Most people who set out to train their cats never perform in public either. Chances are you may not have the patience, the time, or the inclination to teach your cat every trick described in this book. (Your cat may have something to say in that regard, too.) Therefore, what a cat may learn is not what your cat will learn, but rare is the cat who will not learn anything if training sessions are conducted correctly.

Some readers may be satisfied if they can teach their cats not to scratch the furniture and to come when they are called. Other readers, who enjoy walking or who are not comfortable with the idea of keeping their cats indoors all the time, might want to train their cats to walk on a leash. Still other readers who spend a lot of time playing with their cats will want to add variety to that play by teaching their cats to jump through a hoop, fetch, or perform other tricks.

Whatever level of training people choose, it should be a natural

It is never too early to start training your cat, but don't be alarmed if she does not master a trick in one lesson.

When to Begin Training

People obtain their cats in a variety of ways: through free-to-good-homes ads found in newspapers, on supermarket bulletin boards, veterinarians' offices, front lawns, and other locations; by taking a kitten to help out a friend whose unspayed, but should have been spayed, female recently had a litter; from the farmer down the road who always has an extra cat or kitten around; from shelters, pet shops, and breeders; when a pregnant cat takes up residence under the porch; by happening across a foundling kitten abandoned on a city street or country road; or when a cat turns up on the doorstep with a look that says "feed me and I'm yours."

evolution of their relationship with their cats, not the ruination of it. Training is simply another activity that cats and people both enjoy, like napping or watching television together. It is just another game, albeit a more structured one, in the game of cat-keeping life.

Even though a well-behaved cat is its—and its owner's—own reward, training can have unexpected practical uses. One cat owner of my acquaintance had a sick cat that required surgery. While the cat was recovering, its owner and her husband had to put the cat on a table each day to clean his wounds. In short order, they trained the cat to jump onto the table for his medical attention every morning.

When this couple had to go to California, they recorded the words they used to summon their cat, and the cat sitter played that tape when she came over to feed the couple's cats each day. Sure enough, the convalescent cat would appear and jump onto the table as soon as he heard the tape.

No matter how you get a cat or how old it is when you get it, the best time to begin training is as soon as you have established a rapport with the cat. Kittens under two months of age have been trained to perform complex visual-pattern discriminations in laboratory settings. And kittens as young as two months of age can be taught to respond to their names at home. Therefore, as soon as your cat has identified you as the source of food and lavish attention, you should begin teaching her to respond to the name you have chosen for her. (See the Name Game, page 90.)

Chapter 5

The Training-Wheels Chapter

Many children who learn to ride a bicycle start out with a set of training wheels designed to keep them from falling down. Cat trainers need training wheels, too, or else they are faced with the task of reinventing the wheel when they first set out to train their cats. If a cat is not already a well-established functional member of the family, you are in for a bumpy ride if you think you can thrust him right into the spotlight before he is ready. Here is how to get him ready.

Litter-pan Training

Whether you own several cats already or you are planning a welcoming party for your first cat this weekend, there are several elementary principles of litter-pan training with which you should be familiar. Always keep the pan in the same quiet, easy-to-reach place. While your new cat is getting used to his new surroundings, place him gently into the pan after meals, naps, and spirited play to reinforce his instincts. Praise your cat quietly after he has used the pan. Do not allow him to wander far from the litter-pan room unless you are along to supervise. If you leave your cat home alone, confine him to the room in which the litter pan is located.

Dirty pans often can be the cause of accidents. All waste should be scooped out of the pan and disposed of each day. Additional litter should be added as required. Once a week—or sooner if your nose suggests—dump all the litter, wash the pan thoroughly with a mild, nonammonia-based cleaner, rinse well, and put 1 to 2 inches (2.5–5 cm) of fresh litter into the pan.

If your cat is comfortable with one kind of litter, stick with that brand. Cats are creatures of habit as well as cleanliness. Switching litter may upset your cat's routine, which might result in accidents. If you must, for some reason, train your cat to use a new litter, fold a small, unnoticeable amount of the new litter into the old kind at the weekly litter change. On successive weeks, fold increasing amounts of the new litter into the mix until the changeover has been effected.

An Introduction to Grooming

Grooming is the art of removing dead hair from a cat so he does not have to remove it himself. Like virtue, grooming is its own reward. The more dead hair you collect from your cat, the less you have to collect from the furniture, your clothing, and the rugs.

In addition to the contribution it makes to keeping your house company-ready at all times, grooming helps to make your cat training-ready as well. If your cat is used to being groomed regularly and if he finds that association pleasant, he is more apt to take kindly to train-

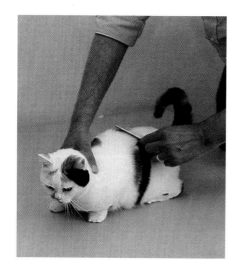

Cats must be trained to accept grooming attention before they can master more complicated assignments.

ing. If your cat is groomed only with the changes of the seasons or if grooming sessions are exercises in full-contact karate, he will not be inclined to sit if you place him on a table and exert a slight downward pressure on his rump while saying "Killer, sit."

A well-behaved cat should not be a stranger to a comb or brush. If your cat is not comfortable being groomed, school should begin as soon as he is settled in his new surroundings. If he has been settled there for several years and you have not established friendly grooming relations, that is the first "trick" you should teach him, grooming him two or three minutes every second or third day until he is used to being handled.

If you do not have a grooming table, and most cat owners do not, a table or a counter in the kitchen or the bathroom will serve your purpose well. Avoid grooming your cat on any surface, the kitchen table, for example, where he is not allowed to venture. If you remove your cat from the table one day then groom him there the next, you could sow confusion in his mind. If there are no tables in your house that the cat is allowed to explore, perhaps you ought to visit a pet shop to price grooming tables.

Before you begin grooming, lay out the tools required for the task. You will need all of the following tools some of the time and some of the following tools all the time:

- comb(s) or brush(es)
- cotton swabs
- face cloth
- nail clippers
- lukewarm water
- mineral oil
- paper cup or other receptacle for dead hair

You need only two combs to keep a shorthaired cat looking smart: a flea comb and a grooming comb with teeth about ⅝-inch (1.6cm) long and ¹⁄₁₆-inch (.2 cm) apart. In some combs the tight, flea-catching teeth occupy half the comb's length while the all-purpose teeth occupy the other half. If you add a third comb to your arsenal, select one whose teeth are closer together than ¹⁄₁₆ inch (.2 cm). No matter what comb you choose, the teeth should be rounded, not pointed, or else they might inflict pain on your cat.

An adequate all-purpose comb for grooming a longhaired cat has teeth that are ⅞-inch (2.2cm) long and are divided into two equal sections. The teeth occupying one half of the comb are almost ³⁄₁₆-inch (.5 cm) apart. The teeth occupying the other half are a little more than one-sixteenth of an inch (.2 cm) apart. A good second comb for longhairs has teeth about ⅝-inch (1.6- cm) long and a little less than ¹⁄₁₆ inch (.2 cm) apart. In addition, some people prefer combs with teeth of alternating length—⅞ inch (2.2 cm) and ¾-inch (1.9 cm)—for grooming longhairs, and others recommend combs with ⅝-inch (1.6cm) long teeth that rotate as they move through the cat's coat because the rotating motion helps to remove dead hair delicately.

Brushes are available in various materials and shapes with bristles made of animal hair, plastic, or stainless steel. The tips of the latter often are covered with tiny, plastic balls. Some brushes have natural bristles on one side and stainless-steel or synthetic bristles on the other. Many people do not like nylon- or plastic-bristle brushes because they damage a cat's coat and generate static electricity, which makes grooming difficult. The same caveat regarding the teeth on a comb applies to the bristles on a brush: The tips of the bristles should not be so sharp as to inflict pain on your cat.

Clipping Your Cat's Claws

Begin each grooming session by checking your cat's claws. With the cat facing away from you, either standing on a table or sitting on your lap, lift one of the cat's legs so that the lower part of the leg rests in your upturned fingers. Holding the leg securely but unthreateningly between the heel of your thumb and the tips of your middle, ring, and little fingers, grasp the cat's foot between your thumb and forefinger. Press down on the top of the

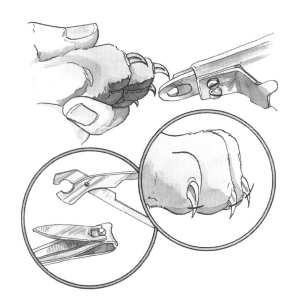

A cat's claws should be clipped regularly. Be careful to clip only the hooked part of the claw. Do not cut into the quick—the visible, pink vein inside the nail.

cat's foot with your thumb, spreading the toes and extending the claws. Check each claw individually. If the end is blunt or rounded, leave it be. If the nail is honed to a talonlike point, clip it. Be careful to clip the hooked part of the claw only. Avoid cutting into the quick—the visible, pink vein inside the nail.

Combing and Brushing Techniques

Because many cats are less amenable to being groomed in some areas (their bellies or hindquarters, perhaps) than they are in others, do not begin with one

of these sensitive zones. Begin instead with a neutral zone such as the back of the neck or the base of the spine.

First, comb or brush in the direction that the coat lies. Slide the comb into the coat at about a 45-degree angle. Do not push down constantly on the comb. Move it across the cat's body smoothly with your wrist locked. This technique also applies if you are using a brush, the only difference being that the bristles of a brush will meet the coat at a 90-degree angle.

With young kittens, and with some older cats, you will need to wield the comb or brush with one hand while you steady the cat with the other. For example, place your free hand on the cat's chest while you comb his back and sides; or place your free hand, palm up, on his underbelly while you comb your pet's hindquarters or neck.

To comb your cat's underbelly, lift his front legs with one hand and comb with the other. Place your free hand, palm up, just behind and above the midpoint of the cat's front legs. Lift his legs gently until he is standing on his hind legs with his back at about a 60-degree angle to the table. This technique is effective if you and the cat are facing the same direction. If the cat is facing you, place your free hand palm down instead of palm up when you lift the cat's front legs.

Cats should be combed twice per grooming session, once to find flea dirt, skin rashes, or mats in the coat, particularly in the "armpits" of the cat's front legs. If you find flea dirt, a flea bath is in order. Skin rashes merit a visit to the veterinarian, who can assess the problem and prescribe treatment. If you encounter a small mat about the size of a marble, do not try to rake it out with the comb or brush. Take the mat in both hands, instead, holding the right half between the thumb and forefinger of your right hand and the left half between the thumb and forefinger of your left hand. Pull tenderly in opposite directions, being careful to pull parallel with your cat's skin. The mat should separate into two, smaller mats. Repeat the procedure, separating the two mats into four. The mats may then be small enough and loose enough to be tugged out carefully, one at a time, with the comb. If they are not, separate them once more and then comb them out.

Do not try to remove an overly large mat with the subdivide-and-conquer method just described. Make an appointment with a professional groomer or a veterinarian and have the mat shaved off.

If you *must* try to remove it, cut the mat with scissors, leaving about ½ inch of mat. Do not try to cut the mat any closer to the skin or you might cut the skin instead. You may then be able to subdivide the mat into small sections that can be teased out with a comb.

To groom your cat's tail, cup it on the underside with one hand about midway along the tail. Comb softly in the direction that the coat lies, moving the comb in 2- or 3-inch (5–7.6 cm) increments from the tip to the base of the tail. To comb the underside of the tail, lift the tail by its tip with one hand and comb in 2- or 3-inch (5–7.6 cm) increments with the lie of the coat as before, working from the tip toward the base of the tail.

If your cat leaps off the table while you are grooming, fetch the cat and return it to the table—even if you were about finished. Retrieving the cat will be easier if you close the doors to the room before you began grooming. After you have returned the fugitive to the grooming table, continue grooming. If you were nearly finished when your cat made his escape, groom for another minute or two anyway. By retrieving your cat and carrying on where you were interrupted, you are letting your pet know that grooming is finished when you say so, not when he does. This lesson will come in handy when you begin training your cat to do tricks.

Bathing Your Cat

Unless they have a close encounter with a skunk, fleas, body mites, or fungus spores, most cats can live happily on regular brushing and/or combing without ever being bathed. Most cat owners, for their part, will live even more happily without ever having to bathe a cat. If you acquired your cat after it had become set in its ways—a condition that sets in around eight months of age—leave well enough and your cat alone and pray that it never needs a bath. And if it does, consult your local groomer.

If you acquired your cat as a young kitten, however, there is no reason why you should not get it used to water by bathing it once every four to six weeks until it gets comfortable with the procedure. The experience may prove beneficial to both of you later in life.

The kitchen sink is the vehicle of choice for most cat baths. A comfortable sink is at least 19 inches (48 cm) wide, 16 inches (41 cm) long, and 6.5 inches (17 cm) deep. Some sinks have built-in spray attachments. If yours does not, buy one at a hardware store, where you also can buy an adapter that will connect any spray attachment to any faucet.

To facilitate bathing, inveigle a spouse or a friend who has just dropped by for coffee to assist in the ceremony. Have a cat carrier nearby with an absorbent towel covering the floor, in case your cat goes ballistic during the bath and needs to dry out before being released.

Before placing your cat in the sink, lay out the implements you will need for the ceremony. These include:

- comb(s) or brush(es) or both
- two terrycloth washcloths
- regular or flea shampoo
- three bath towels
- cotton balls
- eight stacks of prefolded paper towels, about six panels thick
- blunt-tipped scissors
- toothbrush
- two small bowls of lukewarm water
- mineral oil in a squeeze bottle
- mechanic's hand-soap solution (optional)
- dishwashing-detergent solution (optional)
- hair dryer (optional)

After assembling the requisite materials and your determination, cover the bottom of the sink with a rubber mat or a bath towel to provide secure footing for your cat. Before putting your cat into the sink, however, check his claws. If they need clipping, clip them. Some people also wrap a cat's feet and lower legs in masking tape to make sure the claws stay sheathed throughout the bath.

Now check your cat's ears. Remove visible dirt with a cotton swab or cotton ball moistened with hydrogen peroxide or mineral oil. Then put a small wad of cotton in each ear to prevent water from reaching the ear canal and possibly causing infection. Put a few drops of mineral oil in each of the cat's eyes to protect them from stray shampoo.

If your cat's face needs washing, clean it with lukewarm water and a face cloth. More-than-a-little-dirty faces can be cleaned with a weak solution of water and tearless shampoo. Squirt a few drops of shampoo into a bowl of lukewarm water, stir, and, using a washcloth, rub the solution carefully into the soiled areas on your cat's face. Rinse by dipping a clean washcloth into a clean bowl of lukewarm water and rubbing the shampoo out of the fur.

When the moment of immersion is at hand, place your cat in the sink, and let the good times and the water roll. Test the temperature of the water with your wrist. If the water feels uncomfortably warm to you, chances are it may to your cat. Adjust accordingly. Make sure, too, that the house temperature is at least 72°F (22°C).

If you are using flea shampoo on your cat, wet his neck thoroughly at once and lather it well to prevent fleas on the cat's body from hiding out on his face. If your cat's tail is greasy, or if his coat is greasy in any area, take a handful of mechanic's hand-soap solution, rub it into the greasy spot, and work the solution into the coat. (To prepare the degreasing solution, combine half a can of hand soap, which is available at hardware stores, with an equal amount of water and let stand overnight.)

After massaging the hand-soap solution into the greasy area, rinse completely. You are finished rinsing when the water coming off the cat is as clear as the water going onto the cat.

Having degreased any offending spots on your cat, wet him down thoroughly with the spray attachment until he is soaked to the skin. Then apply the dishwashing-detergent solution to the entire coat, lathering the coat generously. Never lather past the cat's neck or you risk getting shampoo in his eyes. Put some shampoo on the toothbrush and brush the shampoo into the hair directly behind the cat's ears.

After your cat has been rinsed clean, apply regular cat shampoo, lathering copiously again. If you use a regular shampoo, rinse your cat after lathering. If you use a flea shampoo, check the label first to see if the manufacturer recommends leaving the shampoo on the coat for a while before rinsing. (A flea bath is only part of the full-frontal assault needed to rid your cat and your house of fleas. Space limitations prevent describing that campaign here. Consult your veterinarian for advice about waging war on fleas.)

There are three secrets to a clean coat: rinse, rinse, and rinse. Some people use a premixed vinegar-and-water solution as a final rinse for optimum soap-scum removal. About half a cup of vinegar in a gallon of water is sufficient. Other people prefer a conditioning rinse manufactured for human use.

After your cat has been rinsed, take hold of his tail at the base with one hand, as if you were gripping a tennis racket, and squeeze gently, coaxing out as much water as you can. Repeat from midpoint to base of tail and on each leg. Blot his legs, tail, and body with paper towels to absorb as much additional moisture as possible. Then remove the cat from the sink and wrap him in a towel, which can be warmed in the oven beforehand for your cat's postbath comfort.

Drying Your Cat

A shorthaired cat in a warm house can be allowed to air-dry after a bath. If you do not want a wet cat sitting on the furniture, confine your pet to the bathroom until he dries. Give him water and food and something with which to amuse himself.

The more special the food treat, the more likely he is to remember that baths end pleasantly. Your cat should be virtually dry in an hour.

Longhaired cats can be allowed to air-dry, too, but often they end up looking like something the cat dragged in. Hair dryers are more efficient and produce better results. If you are going to use a hand-held dryer, put two or three drops of natural-tears solution or another moisturizing agent into your cat's eyes before you begin.

Cats do not take naturally to hair dryers any more than they take naturally to water. The best time to get your cat acclimated to the sound of a hair dryer is before you plan to use it. If you employ a hair dryer on your own hair, bring your cat into the bathroom or bedroom when you dry your hair. If you do not fancy the blow-dried look, run the hair dryer somewhere in the area where you feed your cat. Start the dryer on a low-speed setting before you begin preparing the cat's food. Leave the dryer running while he eats. If he shies at the sound, leave the dryer running and leave the room for a few minutes. If your cat refuses to eat, take up the food, turn off the dryer, and try again in a half hour. Eventually he will get hungry enough to eat with the dryer running.

Before applying the hair dryer, put a towel on the surface your cat will occupy while being dried. Wrist test the temperature of the air coming out of the dryer. The air should not be too hot nor too forceful. The best dryers are the ones with separate speed and temperature controls and quiet-running motors.

Some people begin the drying process by placing their cat in a carrier, the towel-lined one that had been prepared for emergencies. If you try this approach, position the dryer so that warm air blows temperately into the carrier through the front door.

After 20 minutes or so, take your cat out of the carrier and place him on a table or counter. While directing a stream of warm air into his coat, comb cautiously. After the hairs in that area have been separated, move to another area of the cat. If you are attempting this job alone, be sure to use a hair dryer that has a stand into which you can set the dryer, thus leaving your dryer hand free for lifting the cat while you dry and comb his underbelly. Be sure that the dryer stand is resting on a towel, otherwise as soon as you have the dryer adjusted to the proper angle for drying your cat's underbelly, the stand will start moving backward of its own accord.

When you have gone over the entire cat once with the dryer, begin again. This time concentrate on one section of coat at a time. Do not concentrate more than a minute or two on any one section because the heat from the dryer could become uncomfortable for your cat. To avoid this possibility, keep the dryer moving back and forth above the section on which you are working. Use a toothbrush (or a flea comb) to groom your cat's face. If you notice that static electricity is raising cain with his hair, rub a cling-free type anti-static cloth over his coat to smooth the hair into place.

Routine Ear Care

A few cotton swabs or cotton balls and some rubbing alcohol, mineral oil, or hydrogen peroxide in a small container are the only materials you need to clean your cat's ears. Dip the cotton swabs or cotton balls into the alcohol, oil, or peroxide (the choices are yours) and swab the visible parts of the ear carefully. Do not plunge the cotton swab or cotton ball down into the ear canal any farther than the eye can see, or you might do some damage. If you wish to clean your cat's lower ear canal, buy a cleaning solution from your veterinarian and follow the instructions faithfully.

Chapter 6

Basic Cat Training, Part I

The basic training discussed in this and the following chapter need not be the first training a cat receives. Nor do intermediate and advanced training, discussed in Chapters 8 and 9, depend on a foundation established in the two basic-training chapters. In fact, basic training, as defined in this book, is the behavioral opposite of the intermediate and the advanced kind. Basic training is designed to prevent or discourage unwanted behavior, either by modifying a cat's environment or by some sort of reprimand. In basic training the goal is to teach cats not to jump on the kitchen or dining room table, condition their claws on the sofa, break into the trash receptacle, or engage in some other antisocial activity. Intermediate and advanced training are based on positive reinforcement: teaching your cat by means of some reward to perform certain desirable actions, such as coming when you call, walking on a lead, sitting up and begging, or jumping through a hoop.

Because cats are virtually never too young to learn nor too old to start misbehaving, you may begin teaching your cat intermediate lessons, using positive reinforcement, before you find it necessary to provide basic, negative instruction. That need not be a problem if you do not mix the two kinds of training. If, for example, you have just scolded your cat for jumping onto a recessed windowsill and knocking an expensive knickknack to the floor, you should not proceed to get out the treats and begin teaching her to jump through a hoop.

Why Cats Misbehave

Cats' predatory nature and bristling sense of territory have been changed remarkably little by 3,500 years of domestication. Thus, in the back alleys of our cities, the backyards of suburbia, and the backwoods and countryside of rural America, modern-day cats lead singular lives. Low population densities, well-established rituals, limited interaction among adult cats, clearly defined territories, and one-tom-per-neighborhood leasing arrangements characterize the outdoor existence—whose by-laws apply equally to feral (unowned) cats and to household pets that are given outdoor privileges.

In the wild, every cat occupies its own territory. Those territories consist of a home range and a home area. According to one study, the home range is about .3 to 1.2 miles (0.5 to 2 kilometers) in diameter, depending on population density and location. The smaller home area is roughly 111 yards (100 meters) in diameter. The boundaries separating the home range from the home area are not precision etched, nor are the boundaries between one cat's territory and another's. The home range of one cat frequently overlaps that of another cat, especially among male cats, which usually occupy larger home ranges than do females. For their part, however, females defend their territories, particularly their home areas, more fiercely than do males. Males fight for supremacy and rank. Females go to war over territory.

Cats that live in overlapping territories avoid conflict by observing timetables for traveling through or staying in the commonly held portions of their domains. In addition, one cat may defer to another on sight or after inspecting scent marks left on various trees and bushes along trails leading through the overlapping parts of their territories.

Many studies of the social behavior and organization of feral and semiferal domestic cat populations throughout the world have revealed that seldom is the social structure of one group of cats exactly like that of another. For example, females were fang-and-claw territorial in one study and mutually tolerant, cooperative even, in another. Such evidence is further testimony to the cat's one unchanging characteristic: its changeability. Other domestic animals that go feral (revert to living on their own) do not display the social versatility exhibited by cats. Feral horses, cattle, sheep, goats, pigs, and dogs replicate, with varying degrees of exactness, the social systems that have been employed by their wild ancestors for tens of thousands of years.

Obviously, cats that spend most or all of their lives indoors—in

Cats that live indoors are asked to forgo many pleasures. Cat owners, therefore, are challenged to find ways of recapitulating the cat's natural world in an indoor environment.

exchange for regular meals, human companionship, and climate-controlled lodging—are asked to adapt to conditions that violate the established patterns of life on the outside. Indoor cats rule much smaller territories than they would command outdoors; they meet fewer opportunities to exercise their natural instincts; and, in multicat households, they must tolerate greater interaction with other adult cats.

These departures from a cat's natural lifestyle can lead to deviations in behavior such as refusing to use the litter pan, quarreling with other members of the feline brigade, turning the breakfront into

Looking like part of a balancing act, two gentlemen coax a cat down from its perch.

a scratching post, and spraying urine on your favorite chair. Indeed, the more that indoor living stifles the expression of a cat's natural instincts, the greater the chance the cat will misbehave, if "misbehave" is the proper word. For what the cat owner sees as misbehaving, the cat no doubt sees as doing what comes naturally. A cat is an animal, not a miniature person in fur.

The most frequent behavior problem for which cat owners seek professional help for their pets can be described tactfully as inappropriate elimination. Appropriate elimination, of course, occurs in the litter pan. The inappropriate kind occurs somewhere else, especially in places where you might discover it with your bare foot at 2:00 in the morning on your way to the bathroom. Fortunately, the percentage of cats that seek comfort outside their pans is small, probably in the single digits among cats that are neutered or spayed—as all companion cats should be.

Ruffles can forget her manners for a number of reasons: She is suffering from cystitis or some other illness that makes elimination painful or otherwise unpleasant. She has decided that she prefers the feel of a shag carpet or a linoleum floor to that of her litter. Another cat in the house harasses her when she is in the pan. She has grown too large for the pan she has been using since kittenhood. Her pan has not been cleaned for several days. Her pan has been moved to a new location that does not sit well with her. She is playing or sleeping on the second floor and does not feel like going all the way downstairs to relieve herself. You have changed brands of litter, and Ruffles prefers the old brand because the new one does not smell right to her. She does not like the feel of the new litter you bought on sale. She is used to an open pan, and you have switched abruptly to one of those high-tech, enclosed models that looks like an economy-size Toyota. Her pan is located in a part of the house where the traffic pattern does not afford her sufficient privacy. Her pan is situated too close to her dining area or her favorite sleeping spot. She is registering her objection to the new cat or kitten you brought home recently. She is registering a similar objection to a neighbor's cat, whom she sees, from her perch in the living-room window, snooping about on the front lawn.

Remedial Litter-pan Training

Of all the reasons that Ruffles may not be using her pan, the most serious are medical ones. Therefore, says animal behaviorist Daniel Q. Estep, "when a cat stops using the litter pan, you should take the cat to the veterinarian to find out if a medical condition is causing the problem. A lot of medical conditions can

lead to inappropriate elimination. If the problem is medical, most often it's some sort of urinary-tract infection, but other conditions can lead to defecation problems."

If you find tiny urine spots around the house, much smaller than the ordinary volume your cat expresses, she may be suffering from a urinary-tract infection. Older, neutered males are especially prone to this difficulty. Unable to pass urine normally—and uncomfortable from their increasing urinary-tract blockage—they will strain to squeeze out a few drops wherever the urge overtakes them.

Until your cat has been to the vet, you should not assume that the cause of the elimination problem is not medical. What's more, says Estep, "the sooner you get your cat to the vet, the better. Too often people let litter-pan problems go for a long time before they seek help. If it's a medical problem, the cat deserves prompt treatment. If it's a behavioral problem, the cat may establish a habit of not using the pan. Old habits are harder to break than new ones. So the sooner you address a problem, the more likely you are to find a quick solution to it."

The solutions to most litter-pan problems not caused by illness are straightforward. If the adolescent Ruffles has outgrown her pan, buy her a larger one at least 19 x 15 x 4 inches (48.3 x 45.7 x 10.2 cm). If you have let too much time elapse between pan cleanings, resolve to keep the pan more tidy. Remove all waste products, solid or moist, each day and top up the litter as necessary to maintain a constant 1 ½-inch (3.8-cm) to 2-inch (5.1-cm) level. Once a week (or more frequently if your nose or your cat's behavior dictates) discard all the litter in the pan, wash the pan thoroughly with a mild, nonammonia-based cleanser, then rinse, dry, and refill the pan.

If you want to move the litter pan to a new location, put a second pan in that spot and wait until your cat has begun using that pan before taking up the old one. (If your cat resumes eliminating in the spot where the old pan had been located, resign yourself to having two pans in the house.) If your cat is allowed upstairs as well as down, install a litter pan on both levels of the house. If you want to change brands of litter for economic or aesthetic reasons, change gradually. The next time you wash and refill the litter pan, mix two or three cupfuls of the new brand of litter in with the old brand. If your cat does not object, add two or three additional cupfuls of the new brand at the following cleaning. Repeat this gradual infiltration until the transition is complete. If your cat stops using the pan at any time before or immediately after the transition has been accomplished, throw the new litter away, wash and rinse the litter pan, and return to the old brand of litter.

If you want to change from an open pan to an enclosed model, do not fill the new pan with fresh litter. Use the litter that was in your cat's former pan instead. This familiar litter, especially if it is a little soiled, will make the new pan smell homey and reassuring to your cat. Should your cat refuse to set foot in the covered pan, graciously accept the fact that you are stuck with the topless model.

If your cat stops using a pan located in a part of the house that resembles a freeway more than it does a quiet country road, move the pan to a more secluded place. Cats are creatures of decorum as well as habit, and most of them prefer to conduct their private affairs in private.

If you suspect that Ruffles has stopped using her pan because it is too close to her dining or sleeping area, move the pan farther away from that spot. If she begins misbehaving shortly after you have brought a new cat or kitten into the house, provide Ruffles with a new pan at some distance from the old pan's location. (To decrease the possibility that Ruffles will express her displeasure over the new cat's arrival on the sofa or rug, see Training Cats to Accept a New Arrival, page 73.)

Catching Them in the Act

The solutions just discussed are wonderfully painless and cheerfully manipulative and should serve to rehabilitate your cat if she forgets her manners. In addition, catching your cat in violation of house rules and reprimanding her promptly can be effective, but a reprimand is only as effective as it is timely. A cat's correction span—that is, the length of time during which she will associate a correction with the act that inspired and directly preceded that correction—is three to five seconds long at most. Therefore, it serves little purpose, other than venting your frustration, to find Ruffles, drag her to the spot where she misbehaved, and scold her for something she did fifteen minutes, thirty minutes, or two hours ago. Should you catch her in the act, express your annoyance with a sternly spoken *No, bad kitty.* You may substitute the expletive of your choice for kitty, but bad and no should be part of your respective vocabularies.

Punishment after the fact is counterproductive, says Estep. "We always tell our clients, 'If you don't catch the animal in the act, don't even think about punishing it.' That punishment is not going to affect behavior, and it is likely to create a further problem because the animal will become fearful of its owner, which could affect a person's bond with an animal.

"Yet many people whose cats have soiled the house or have been destructive in some way will take the cat to the place where it misbehaved and punish it. These people think the cat will know what it has done wrong and will learn not to do it again. But animals don't learn that way. What a cat will learn from that sort of punishment is to associate its mess and the presence of the owner with unpleasantness. The cat will infer that something bad is going to happen if its owner comes through the door when there's a mess in the house. So the cat figures it had better run. Or it may show submissive behavior. People then wrongly assume that the cat looks guilty because it knows it has done something wrong. They further assume, wrongly again, that their punishment must have been effective."

Instead of rubbing your cat's nose in any mess she has made, clean the soiled spot with a nonammonia-based disinfectant cleaner. If Ruffles has dirtied the carpet, sprinkle white distilled vinegar and salt on it to expunge the odor. Do not use an ammonia-based cleanser to clean urine because ammonia smells too much like the odor you are trying to remove, and Ruffles will be likely to return to this spot like a heat-seeking missile in the future.

Tales of Two Kitties

Fortunately, most litter-pan rebellions are short-lived and most are easily remedied, with a little ingenuity. The tales of two kitties of my acquaintance, Bummy and Willard, illustrate this point.

Bummy's tale begins one early spring night. My wife Mary Ann and I, having seen some guests to the door, were about to turn off the lights in the kitchen when we noticed several cats staring in horror at a large bowl of dry food sitting on the floor. While the cats mumbled ominously to one another, I went to see what was the matter.

The matter, which should have been deposited in a litter pan, was sitting like a perverse, double-scoop creation in the middle of the bowl of dry food. Newly minted and still malodorous, the matter constituted a source of great offense to the adult members of the feline community. . . and a source of some amusement to Mary Ann and me. We restored the dry-food bowl to its former hygienic condition and retired for the evening still speculating about which of the five eight-week-old kittens in the house had slipped its moorings.

The answer was not forthcoming immediately, though the perpetrator struck again several times during the next few days. After spending more time than normal people ought to spend monitoring the personal habits of their kittens, we were sitting in the living room one night when we heard an indignant howl in the kitchen. We went to investigate and saw a red tabby kitten named Bum's Rush poised significantly in the dry-food bowl. An adult male named Doughboy stood next to the bowl, sternly rebuking the preoccupied Bummy.

Once the mystery had been solved, the remedy was simple: switch to a smaller dry-food bowl, one too small to accommodate even a kitten. Why, you may ask, had we not hit upon that solution sooner? Because no matter how long we live with cats, we humans often take longer than we should to remember that we are just as smart as they are.

Another problem child of our acquaintance was a neutered red Persian male named Willard, who developed what animal behaviorists call "a surface preference" regarding his place of elimination. The surface Willard preferred to litter for solid-waste deposits was carpet. Litter was fine for liquid waste, but for really big jobs Willard got down and dirty on the rug. Luckily, the problem seemed to come and go, much as Willard did; and he would revert to using his pan for weeks at a time after one or two misdeeds, particularly if he was caught redhanded.

When we moved to a new house, however, Willard overreacted. He began defecating exclusively at the end of a downstairs hallway. Because the carpet in the hallway was worn—and because it was a hideous green color—I decided, in a fit of Promethean frustration, that it would be easier to pull the carpet up than to continue cleaning up after Willard. That is when I discovered that beneath the hallway carpet lay a handsome hardwood floor.

Willard struck next in the corner of the first-floor bedroom. After a week or two of putting up with that nonsense, I snatched up an end of the bedroom carpet and began pulling. A few hours of furniture moving and fervent cursing later, there was a hardwood floor in the bedroom, too. This one needed a little buffing and polishing, but no big deal.

And none to Willard, either. He simply moved his act to the living room. But the Grim Remover soon followed, and before long there were no carpets on the first floor of the house or on the stairs leading to the second floor or on the landing at the top of the stairs. Because the kitchen and bathroom had tile floors and the doors to the upstairs rooms were kept closed, Willard grudgingly confined his deposits to the litter pan for the next seven years before kidney failure took him to his big, carpeted reward in the sky.

When the Going Gets Tough

Although tearing up the carpet room by room to foil a cat's surface preference has a swashbuckling, thunder-from-the-gods ring about it, most people are probably more fond of their carpets than I was of mine. And truth be known, I would have looked the fool if Willard had been abstaining from his pan for some other reason. The more prudent approach to getting your cat back on the elimination track, once you have determined that the cause of his derailment is not medical, is to analyze the problem before you act.

"We have a whole set of questions we ask about the pattern in which the inappropriate behavior occurs," says Estep. "Does it occur in particular locations in the house? At particular times? For example, if

To Willard's surprise, each time he soiled the carpet, more of it disappeared.

you see a pattern of urination only around windows and doors where other cats have been seen in the past or if it seems to occur right after a cat has a fight with another cat in the house (or with a cat outdoors), that suggests a marking problem rather than a surface-preference or other kind of problem."

There are other clues to look for as well. If a cat does not like the feel of its litter, it will not spend much time digging in its pan. When their feet hit the sand, most cats will dig, some demurely, others demoniacally, before and after eliminating. The amount and the pace of digging vary greatly from one cat to the next, but the cat that jumps into a pan, eliminates, then jumps out and races off without digging at all may be voting with its feet. So may the cat that stands in the pan and scratches at the wall or that jumps out of the pan and starts pawing at the floor. Because this behavior may indicate a blossoming aversion to the litter in the pan, you have nothing to lose by replacing that litter with a different sort (see page 64). If you are using a clay litter, for example, switch to a finer, more sandlike variety.

You also might consider setting up another litter pan with the different kind of litter in it in another part of the house. If your cat becomes a faithful communicant in the new pan with its new litter, you have several options. Put the new litter in the old pan, and if the cat starts using that pan again, take up the new one. Or you might take up the old pan, period. Finally, you might leave both pans, with the new litter in each of them, where they are.

Cats that develop a preference for a nonlitter surface present a greater challenge. Suppose that Willard, bless his carpet-loving soul, had developed a strong preference for carpets to the total exclusion of his pan and that yanking up all the carpets was not an option. What might we have done to solve the problem?

Having determined that Willard's was not a medical problem, that his pan was always clean, that he was not fighting with other cats in the house—in short, that his was more than likely a surface-preference problem—we might have changed types of litter, from clay to sand, from scented to unscented, or vice versa. If that failed, we might have lined the litter pan with carpet remnants that could be washed or replaced regularly. Sprinkling a thin, ¼-inch (0.6-cm) dusting of litter on top of the carpet might have allowed one remnant to be used longer between washings.

If a cat develops a preference for a slick surface instead of litter, a linoleum remnant in the bottom of the pan with a ¼-inch (0.6-cm) covering of litter is indicated. The slick surface preferred by some cats is the bathtub's. In that case, leave an inch or two (2.5 to 5.1 cm) of water in the tub at all times and make the

litter pan more tublike by leaving it empty or by lining the bottom of the pan with linoleum covered by a touch of litter.

The Last Resort

Persons who raise kittens often keep a mother cat and her youngsters in a large cage, roughly 44 inches (111.8 cm) long, 22 inches (55.9 cm) wide, and 22 inches (55.9 cm) tall. The cage is outfitted with a nesting box at one end and a litter pan at the other, and the top of the cage is left open, allowing the mother cat to jump in and out as she desires. When the kittens are four weeks old or so and have begun to find their way to the pan, the cage door may be left open for short periods of supervised free time. This permits the kittens to explore their immediate surroundings outside of the cage while testing their litter-pan instincts.

The kitten that begins to relieve itself outside the cage can begin learning what *No* means at that point. Before long kittens become trustworthy enough to be allowed longer and longer periods of free time. They should still remain in their cage at night for a while, but by the time they are nine or ten weeks old, they will be reliable enough to have the run of the room where their pan is located—generally their owner's bedroom.

This routine sometimes works to rehabilitate a cat that does not respond to less regimented forms of remedial litter-pan instruction. If you have not switched brands of litter suddenly, changed from an open to an enclosed pan, forgotten to clean your cat's litter pan for a week, had company of whom your cat disapproved, or committed any other transgressions, and your cat still refuses to use the pan consistently, you might consider borrowing or buying a large cage in which to confine the cat during rehabilitation. A pet shop may carry this kind of cage; if not, cat magazines contain ads from companies that sell them. The cost of such a cage, under $100, may be less than the cost of having a rug or sofa cleaned professionally. What's more, a large cage is useful when you need to isolate cats that are sick.

Once you have acquired a cage for your miscreant, place cat and

There are great variations in training, background, and experience among cat behaviorists. Always ask for references and, if possible, always consult a certified animal behaviorist if you decide to seek help in solving your cat's behavior problems.

pan in it and leave them there, with food, water, and a toy or two, until the cat is using the pan consistently. To aid in this rehabilitation, dab a few drops of ammonia cut with water on the bottom of the pan before you fill it with litter. The similarity between the odors of urine and ammonia may inspire the desired conduct in your cat.

During rehabilitation, allow your cat out for half an hour or so of supervised recess a few times a day. Increase the free time gradually until the cat exhibits dependability in the confinement room, then allow your pet the run of the house. Be sure to leave the old pan in its former location and the new pan in the confinement room. If your cat uses both pans consistently without misadventure, the price you pay for retraining may be an extra litter pan to look after. A small price for feline cleanliness. You could try taking up the new pan once order has been restored to your cat's litter habits. If accidents begin once more, restore the new pan to the confinement room.

We used the last-resort method with a neighborhood stray whom we adopted several winters ago and ultimately named Prince Ruprecht after a character in *Dirty, Rotten Scoundrels.* When we first brought the yet unnamed Ruprecht indoors, we isolated him in the living room and gave him a pan to use. Ruprecht used the sofa instead. If he was going to remain indoors on winter nights after he had recovered from being neutered, he was going to have to clean up his act. We tried the last-resort method, outfitting Ruprecht's cage with a bed, food, water, and a pan.

When we checked on him in the morning, he was sleeping on the floor of the cage. The pan and the bed had been unused. Apparently he would have to learn the purpose of both. Since there was no sign of misbehavior in the cage and since Ruprecht was meowing earnestly at us, we opened the cage door, then the front door, and he scampered out into the bushes.

We brought Ruprecht in each night for nearly a week before he discovered that the cat bed was more comfortable than the cage floor. Because he still had not solved the riddle of the pan, we continued to let him out each morning. If he came back during the day and we had the time, we would sit with him in the living room. We always left his cage door open in case he would be struck by a sudden inspiration to use the pan.

One day we left him in the living room unattended for some reason, and when we returned, there was a wet spot in the pan. We decided to give Ruprecht the run of the living room that night. Sure enough, when morning had broken, there was another wet spot in the pan and a carefully buried mound of solid waste.

Once he learned what the pan was about, Ruprecht became quite devoted to it. To this day, whenever we clean his pan, he races over as soon as we are finished and christens it promptly. That is how he earned his name. If you have seen *Dirty, Rotten Scoundrels,* you will understand why.

Although the last-resort method worked with Ruprecht, who had never lived indoors before, and it has worked with a few young kittens, it should be the last, not the first resort when most cats misbehave. "The first step, always, is to determine the reason for the problem," says animal behaviorist Suzanne Hetts, PhD.

"If a cat has a preference for carpet, and you confine that cat to a separate room or to a cage where the only elimination choices are the pan and the linoleum floor, the cat might use the pan because it is preferable to linoleum. But as soon as that cat is released from confinement, she is probably going to start using the carpet again because litter reverts to second place." If the last resort and all other at-home resorts have failed, "sometimes we have to rely on working with the owner's veterinarian to put the cat on short-term drug therapy in conjunction with behavior modification," says Hetts.

Cats often spray their urine to attract members of the opposite sex and to mark territory. Although unneutered males are most likely to employ this sort of marking, neutered males, intact females, and spayed females will do so, too, on occasion. Sometimes that occasion is inspired by a cat they have spied through the window. If you can keep your cat out of that window by closing the door to the room where the window is located, you can solve the problem easily.

Cats that spray to mark territory because they are at odds with other cats in the house present a greater challenge. "This kind of spraying is not just a matter of one cat marking off one bedroom and another cat marking off another one," says Estep. "Sometimes the pattern doesn't make a whole lot of sense to humans because the cats are marking here and there and every other place."

When fighting occurs, owners should try to determine its cause. Are the cats fighting over a preferred resting place? A toy? Food? If so, providing an additional resting place, more toys, or more food in a

Cats should not be granted sofa privileges until they have learned to use a scratching post reliably.

separate dish may solve the problem—if you are lucky.

But, cautions Hetts, "Fighting between two cats in the same household doesn't have to be all-out war. It could just be a low-level tension that's always there. In this sort of conflict cats don't actually fight, but they don't like each other either."

Owners who have cats that do not get along have to develop peacemaking skills. "The basic idea is to try to countercondition the cats," says Estep. "That means teaching them a behavior that's counter to the aggressive behavior."

Counterconditioning begins with separation analogous to that employed when introducing a new cat to an existing resident (see page 73). For counterconditioning, however, each of the warring parties should be placed in a separate room so there is no chance of continuing hostilities from opposite sides of a well-marked door. You need not cage the combatants in their rooms unless one is marking all the time.

To recondition the cats, take one to the other's room for short, supervised periods of interaction. If the cats tolerate one another without becoming aggressive, reinforce their behavior with food, petting, or play. The positive reinforcement may help each cat to associate the presence of the other cat with good feelings.

Whatever reinforcement you employ, be careful to apply it equally, and be careful to reward only displays of calm, relaxed behavior. If the cats show signs of aggression, if they tense up, start to hiss, or puff out their tails, separate them and do not reward them.

If your counterconditioning therapy works, allow the cats the run of the house again, but do not spring them unless you or someone else in your family is going to be home to monitor their behavior. If counterconditioning does not result in a truce and in a cessation of spraying, the situation may require the attention of a certified animal behaviorist and/or short-term, anti-anxiety drug therapy supervised by a veterinarian.

Though it may seem heretical for the author of a book on cat training to acknowledge that some situations defy fixing, they do. Should two of your cats take such an instant or a long-simmering hatred to one another that their animosity puts them at physical risk, consider placing one of them in a home where he or she will be the only cat. This is easier said than accomplished, but it is sometimes the only humane solution to a behavior problem.

Training a Cat to Accept a New Arrival

If you decide to add a cat to your household, bring the new cat home on a weekend or a holiday when you have plenty of time to spend with her and with your present cat. Before you bring the new cat home, prepare a room where she will spend some time in isolation. Do not select the old cat's favorite sanctuary or resting place for this purpose. The idea is to fit the new cat into the old cat's routine, not to make the old cat feel dethroned.

Solitary confinement is recommended for the new cat, no matter how current the old cat's vaccinations are or how well the new cat passed her veterinary exam. Until you are satisfied that the new cat is not harboring any illnesses that did not show up during the vet inspection—that is, for ten days to two weeks—she should have no direct and prolonged contact with the old cat. She should, of course, have plenty of visits from you, and you should disinfect your hands thoroughly after each visit.

For the first few days allow the cats to sniff, and perhaps hiss, at each other from either side of a closed door. Admittedly, infectious diseases can be spread by such incidental contact, and some diseases are airborne, but isolation will curtail the spread of infection that occurs when cats use the same litter pan, eat or drink from the same bowl, and lick or bite each other. Thus, the isolation advice is given in the belief that half an ounce of protection is better than none.

When you feel the time is right—and after you have clipped both

The lion, miniature variety, lies down with the lamb, canine representative.

cats' claws—put the new cat into a cat carrier, open the door to her room, and allow the old cat in for a ten-minute visit. Be sure to take up the new cat's water bowl, food dish, and litter pan first.

Repeat these daily visits until any hissing, growling, or back arching subsides, then allow the cats unfettered, but supervised, contact. Bring the old cat into the isolation ward, but this time do not confine the new cat beforehand. Put the old cat on the floor, retire to a neutral corner, and have a blanket, a pan of cold water, and a broom handy. All should go well, but if the rare, life-threatening fight erupts, use the pan of water and/or the broom to separate the combatants, and throw the blanket over the nearest pugilist. While the cat is wriggling around underneath the blanket, pick up blanket and cat and return the latter to its original territory.

After a day or so, reinstate the brief visitations. A few days after

Cats observe certain rituals when greeting one another. In addition to scoping out the youngster, the adult cat is seeking permission to enter the young one's personal air space.

that, attempt the free-range introduction again. Do not fret if the cats refuse to curl up together in a corner. The best they may achieve is a distant but tolerant relationship.

Scratching the Right Surface

Cats scratch for two reasons: to remove the dead, outer husks from their claws and to mark territory, both visually and with scent from glands in their paws. Whatever their motivation, however, cats are without consciences regarding the surfaces into which they sink their claws. Like children of the 1960s, cats will scratch wherever and whenever it feels good; and like good parents of any decade, cat owners must concentrate their cats' scratching behavior on surfaces that cat and owner find mutually acceptable. Most owners prefer that those surfaces be wrapped around a scratching post.

A scratching post is better than Scotch Guard for protecting furniture, but all scratching posts are not created equal. The physically correct post should be well anchored so that it will not tip over when a cat uses it. The post also should be tall enough so that cats can stretch themselves while scratching. The scratching surface should be made from a strong, stalwart material like sisal or hemp. Finally, the scratching post should be installed in your house before you install your cat, thereby enabling you to show your cat where the post is—and what it is there for—after you have shown her to the litter pan. (Like litter pans, scratching posts should be deployed—at least one to a story—on every story of your house to which your cat has access.)

Cat owners can lessen the amount of husk-removal scratching their cats engage in by seeing that the cats' claws are clipped regularly. (See Clipping Your Cat's Claws, page 53.) Clipping removes the tip of the claw and, in the bargain, the husk of dead claw, if there is one, covering the fresh, sharper claw underneath. If their claws are clipped once a week or so, as needed, cats will have less need to remove the husks of dead claws by scratching—an activity frequently mistaken for sharpening the claws.

Yet no matter how attentive you are to Ruffles' claws, she still will want a good scratch now and again if for no other reason than because it feels so good to stretch her muscles in the process. Clipping is about as fruitful as tugging on Superman's cape to prevent that sort of exercise scratching. Fortunately, it need not be prevented. Redirecting your cat's attention to a scratching post will mollify you and Ruffles as well.

To teach Ruffles to use a scratching post, wave a toy directly in front of it so that Ruffles' nails dig into the post as she grabs for the toy. Two or three times after realizing how good it feels to sink her claws into the post, she will get the idea. Then wave the toy farther up the post so that she is encouraged to climb up after the toy. Play this game two or three times a day for a few days and Ruffles soon will be climbing the post as though a neighborhood dog were in agitated pursuit.

Because cats have scent glands in their paws, scratching leaves a cat's signature on whatever the cat scratches. This phenomenon works to an owner's benefit with scratching posts. The more a post reminds a cat of herself, the more she will be inclined to return there, cats being more than a little narcissistic.

Cats also scratch to mark territory, and this kind of scratching is most likely to occur near places where cats sleep, near entrances to rooms, or in areas where cats see or encounter other cats. If you allow your cat to sleep on your $2,000

Corinthian-leather sofa, you should not blame her if she takes a few divots out of the sofa upon waking—no matter how closely you have stationed a scratching post.

If that sofa is near a window through which Ruffles can see the next door neighbor's cat having a BM on your lawn, Ruffles is liable to scratch the sofa by way of showing the offending cat whose lawn that is and warning her to take her business elsewhere. If such is the case, you could move the sofa, board up the window, lock up your neighbor's cat, or deny Ruffles access to the living room, library, or den in which your slowly disintegrating sofa is located.

Wherever your cat is doing her delinquent scratching, you should consider the scene of the crime as Lieutenant Columbo or Jessica Fletcher would—by asking a number of questions. Is there a scratching post in the area where the unde-

Hanging 18, this cat poses on a surfboard made of driftwood.

sirable scratching is perpetrated? What about the object Ruffles is using instead of her post? Is it more coarse than the scratching post? Or is it more soft and yielding? Is the object horizontal or vertical?

If there is no post in the crime-scene area, put one there—as close as possible to the violated surface—and teach Ruffles how to use the post. (See page 75.) If there is a post nearby already, perhaps you should remove its surface covering and replace it with a material more closely resembling the rug or sofa on which Ruffles has been scratching instead. Or perhaps you should not replace the covering at all if Ruffles has been working out on a table leg. If the unwanted scratch marks indicate that Ruffles prefers a low-to-the-floor or an on-the-floor scratching surface (some cats crouch when they scratch) install a suitably configured, horizontal scratching post in that area.

In addition to giving Ruffles a safe-scratching alternative to the surface on which she has been scratching illicitly, you should make that forbidden surface as unappealing as possible by covering it with double-sided sticky tape, aluminum foil, a sheet of sandpaper, or a plastic carpet runner, pointy side up. You might also attach cotton balls soaked in muscle-rub oint-

ment or some other unpleasant-smelling medium to the surface you want her to avoid.

Keep the new post as close to the former crime scene as possible, and keep the scratching deterrents on the inappropriate objects until Ruffles uses the new scratching post without fail for two weeks. Then remove the coverings or scents gradually.

If a scratching post next to the living-room sofa offends your decorator's sensibilities, once Ruffles has returned to the straight and narrow—or to the horizontal and wide—gradually move the post, a foot or so at a time, to a location in the room with which you and your decorator can live.

Chapter 7

Basic Cat Training, Part II

"The true art of government," said Jonathan Shipley, "consists in not governing too much." This worthy advice also applies to basic cat training. Instead of trying to impress upon your cat a long, tedious list of *don'ts*—don't scratch the sofa, don't eat the African violets, don't play soccer with the knickknacks, don't swing from the drapes, don't, don't, don't—establish a few, simple rules your cat will understand and, most of the time, follow. In addition, provide enough diverting amusements to prevent your cat from becoming bored.

The Mischief-proof Environment

Because it is easier to modify a cat's environment in many cases than it is to modify his behavior, the best way to keep cats out of mischief is to keep mischief out of cats' reach. The well-behaved cat is most often the cat with the fewest opportunities to misbehave. Thus, if there

are rooms in the house you do not want your cat to explore, keep the doors to those rooms closed. If there are fragile objects in the rooms your cat is allowed to visit, put them out of climbing range. Make sure all balconies are enclosed, all window screens are secured, and all electrical cords are intact. If your cat or kitten begins teething on electrical cords, wrap them in heavy tape or cover them with plastic tubes, which you can buy in an auto-supply store. If necessary, unplug all appliances that are not in use until you are certain your cat has not developed a taste for electrical cords. To keep your cat from getting a charge out of

Your cat can enjoy the scenery without becoming part of it if you make sure that all window screens in your house are secure.

*If you have
a yen for
delicate
objects, you
should not
allow your
cat to get too
near them.*

electrical sockets, cover them with plastic, plug-in socket guards, which you can buy at the hardware store.

Keep all kitchen and bathroom cleansers, chemicals, cleaners, and toilet articles in cabinets that can be closed or locked securely. Keep the lids on all trash receptacles tightly closed. Consider replacing trash containers whose swing-open

*The cat-proof
house does
not harbor
disasters
waiting for
a cat to sail
in and make
them happen.
How would you
cat-proof the
space above.*

lids could be dislodged—and whose contents could be disgorged—if your cat overturns the containers. (Another lid to keep shut is the toilet-seat lid.)

When closing any door in your house—the front door, back door, refrigerator door, closet door, the door on the clothes washer or dryer—be sure your cat is not on the wrong side. Keep the bathroom door closed when you are filling the tub. When cleaning, rinse all cleansers and chemicals thoroughly from any surfaces on which a cat could walk. What gets on a cat's paws usually winds up in his stomach.

Put sewing supplies and yarn away when you are finished using them. Do not leave rubber bands, hot irons, cigarettes, plastic bags, or pieces of string or yarn lying about. Learn to think like a cat. Look for any potential accident—tinsel on a Christmas tree, a dangling tablecloth, a hot burner on the stove— waiting for a cat to make it happen.

Finally, keep poisonous plants out of reach. Poinsettia, philodendron, caladium, dieffenbachia, English ivy, hydrangea, Jerusalem cherry, mistletoe, and holly are some of the plants poisonous to cats. Ask your veterinarian for a complete list.

Virtuous Alternatives

The privilege of keeping cats— and it is a privilege, not a right—is accompanied by the responsibility of keeping them healthy and content. If you do not want Toby climbing the drapes, you must provide him with something he can climb. If you do not want Toby scratching the sofa, you must provide him with something into which he can sink his claws. If you do not want Toby eating the houseplants, you must provide him with homegrown grasses for nibbling. In short, you must be creative enough to find ways of recapitulating a cat's natural world in an artificial indoor environment—providing toys that inspire hunting and chasing, cat "trees" that extend an opportunity to climb, secluded areas that furnish privacy, and windows that afford an opportunity to observe the world from which indoor cats are excluded. In addition, catnip for the occasional high and comfortable beds for sleeping all should be part of the indoor cat's environment.

Cats play their own brand of chess, which involves moving as many pieces as they can at one time.

something the cat does not associate with you. First, because you do not want your cat to be afraid of you. Second, because you do not want him to refrain from unwanted behavior only when you are in the neighborhood. Moreover, if your cat associates punishment with you and that association makes him afraid of you, that could affect your relationship with him.

Aversive Training

No matter how mightily you strive to make your house mischief proof, your cat will engage in behavior from time to time that you will want to modify. When he does, the best way to effect that modification is to establish in his little cat mind an association between the unwanted conduct and an unpleasant occurrence. If possible, the unpleasant occurrence should be

Two mad hatters pause in their investigation of a hatbox.

79

Putting the Bite on Random Chewing

If you discover your cat nibbling on the leaves of a plant in the living room, you are served better by creating a negative experience for the cat—by squirting him with a water pistol, for example—than by removing him from the plant site and saying "no." If you squirt Toby with a water pistol—provided, of course, you do not announce yourself as the squirter by shouting at him before you do—he will associate the plant with the negative experience of getting wet. If he makes enough associations like that, eventually he will leave the plant alone.

The squirt-gun technique is limited in its application. For it to be effective, you have to camp out in the living room, gun in hand, every time Toby is visiting there. Eternal vigilance may be the price of free-

A cat posing with several trophies. All that are missing are the pith helmet and the rifle.

dom, but a well-behaved cat need not be such a costly investment. Better to create another negative experience for which the plant will get the blame. To do this, apply Bitter Apple, Sour Grapes, Tabasco sauce, or any other nasty-tasting but nontoxic substance to the leaves of the plant. This dash of prevention is worth more than a squirt of cure.

Relying on punishment alone to solve a behavior problem after it has occurred is generally less effective than using a negative experience to prevent the behavior from happening. Besides, if Toby has a strong attraction to a certain plant, he might risk a soaking to nibble on its leaves occasionally; and if you are not there to administer the soaking, he will keep on nibbling. But if the plant leaves a bad taste in his mouth every time he starts snacking on it, he soon will leave the plant alone.

Some people do not approve of using a squirt gun or a foul-tasting substance to persuade a cat to refrain from an unwanted behavior. If these methods make you uneasy, you could close the doors to the rooms where Toby menaces your plants, you could keep only hanging plants in your house, or you could grow some greens for Toby to chew on and show him to those greens every time you find him nibbling on forbidden fronds. In fact, you should provide homegrown treats for Toby to chew on no matter what method you use to keep him away from your plants.

Taste-aversion therapy also puts the bite on other forms of unsanctioned chewing around the house. If your cat develops a taste for the corners of the sofa cushions or the bedspread, season them with Bitter Apple or Tabasco. The same applies to the corners of books or magazines, your slippers, bathroom towels, and any other objects you do not want your cat to chew.

Some trainers have advised cat owners to smear Tabasco sauce on their cats' gums to show the cats how unpleasant it tastes at the same time they (the owners) smear Tabasco on various objects the cat is not supposed to chew. What's more, cat owners have been advised to take an object that a cat has chewed and ruined, spread Tabasco sauce on it "really heavily," and stuff the object into the cat's mouth. This advice, in addition to bordering on the sadistic, violates one of the principal canons of cat training because it constitutes punishment after the fact. A cat whose sensitive mouth tissues have just been scorched is not going to make the necessary connections between the chewing he did and the cruel and unusual punishment he received. Besides, if the object is already ruined, it is beyond saving. And so is any cat owner who would be foolish enough to follow this advice. If there is anything priceless and irreplaceable in your house that could be destroyed if your cat chews it, make sure that object is beyond your cat's reach.

No Panhandling Allowed

Begging is the easiest trick for a cat to learn and the most difficult trick to unlearn. Once Toby has been rewarded for soliciting a bite of your tofu hot dog, you will have created a furry little monster. Expect to find this monster hovering about at mealtimes, a resolute mendicant, all eyes and appetite.

If you do not want Toby nosing around your plate or potato-chip bag, you must discourage him each and every time he does. Without fail. What is done is not easily undone once you begin feeding a cat out of your hand.

On the other hand, "cats can be taught not to beg," says Nancy Kobert, who with her husband, Michael, operates Kobert Animal Productions in Ramona, California. "To stop that kind of behavior I put the flat of my hand on the cat's forehead. I don't hit him, but I push a little bit and go 'hiss.' That's a natural way of telling the cat to back off. That's what they do to each other."

Because cats are inclined to interpret any push, no matter how slight, as an aggressive action, you need not be overly enthusiastic in delivering this message. "You don't want to scare the cat away," Kobert warns. "You just want to call on its natural instinct to back down to a more dominant cat. As soon as you do this, watch your cat's body. He goes into that 'oooh' posture, and the body drops back even if it's only a few centimeters."

Kobert refines this training by rewarding a cat once he is sitting quietly and is no longer showing a fervid interest in her food. Thus she gets to enjoy her cat's company and her victuals at the same time. If you think you can manage this with your cat, fine; but if you simply want your cat to let you eat your cheese doodles in peace, forget the reward.

Jumping to Conclusions

You are sitting at the kitchen table one morning with only your favorite section of the newspaper between you and the day's burdens. You are about to sink a spoon into your grapefruit when Toby jumps onto the table to investigate. With a restrained economy of motion, you rap your spoon sharply against the side of your bowl. If you are using the best china that morning, you could substitute a twenty-mule-team foot stomp. No matter what its source, if the sound you make is startling

enough, Toby should beat feet immediately to lower ground.

You could probably achieve the same response by rattling the newspaper, smacking the underside of the table with your fist, or making any abrupt, unsettling noise. If you happen to be wearing a whistle that morning, an extended blast or two will work nicely.

Do not swat at Toby with your hand, leap up gesticulating like a dictator, or make any other sudden, aggressive motion toward him. If you strike him accidentally, you may make him hand shy, which could interfere with intermediate and advanced training sessions. If you rise up menacingly from the table, bellowing mightily and snorting fire, he will certainly leap off the table and race out of the room, but he also may begin racing out of the room any time he is in the kitchen and sees you getting up from the table.

Although cats are sensitive enough to cease and desist when they are startled, they are curious enough to return to the scene of a misdemeanor. Do not be discouraged, therefore, if Toby lands in the middle of the breakfast table the morning after he was startled off by the clang of spoon on china or the stomp of foot on floor. Be prepared to repeat whatever measure it was that ran him off the first day, and be prepared to escalate the war of wills if necessary—even if it means coming to the breakfast table armed with a squirt gun or a whistle each morning.

It should go without saying, which is probably why it needs to be said, that there is a difference between creativity and cruelty in training a cat. If, when your cat jumped onto the breakfast table, you grabbed him by the scruff of the neck and dunked his nose into a steaming cup of coffee, he probably would refrain from jumping on the table again. He also might burn his nose. He surely would lose faith in you. And he most likely would be unwilling to come when you called or to respond to any positive kind of training.

Getting Toby off the table once he already has beamed himself up is quickly accomplished. Getting him to refrain from jumping on the table altogether takes better timing. To accomplish this, the well-trained owner anticipates the cat's arrival, sees him skulking around the table, and makes a loud noise or barks "no" as soon as he or she spies the cat going into a preleap crouch.

Though you make enough noise to frighten the bejumpers out of your cat, you should keep your corrections impersonal. That is best achieved by not taking your cat's actions personally. He did not jump on the table in order to get your goat. So do not give it to him. All he wanted was to find out what was going on up there, and all you want is a cat-free kitchen table.

The best time to determine what you want from your cat is before he starts doing what you do not want.

"If people decided before they brought their cats into the house what places were going to be off limits and were consistent in enforcing those rules, they would have greater success teaching their cats not to jump onto certain places," says Daniel Q. Estep, "An established habit is difficult to break."

Your cat will be less apt to chew your plants if you give her a plant of her own to nibble.

Training Aids?

Whistles and squirt guns are but two of the low-tech options in the cat trainer's arsenal. The smart-bomb equivalents in the campaign for a well-behaved cat include the Scat Mat, the Tattle Tale, and the Snappy Trainer.

The Scat Mat is a flexible vinyl mat strategically impregnated with electrical wires that plugs into a standard wall socket. When properly engaged and turned on, this bit of ingenuity, available in 30 x

16-inch (76.2 x 40.6-cm) or 20 x 48-inch (50.8 x 121.9-cm) models, delivers what is advertised as "a harmless shock" whenever your cat lands on it. This "harmless shock" has been likened, by a human observer, to the sensation experienced by a person who stands up and tries to walk on a leg that has fallen asleep. Cats describe the "harmless shock" in different terms—terms that, unfortunately, cannot be included in a family publication.

Scat Mats can be deployed on tables, on furniture, and in windowsills; and when they have given Toby all the harmless shocks his psyche can handle, they could be used to enliven any party. Just slip one under a slipcover and watch your guests scream with delight when a preoccupied victim leaps up and spills a drink all over himself. Some fun, hunh?

The Tattle Tale, a small plastic device that comes with batteries included, is alleged to keep dogs and cats away from furniture, plants, countertops, and other surfaces. "The slightest movement activates a distinct 2 second (sic) alert to inform you of a disturbance," says one supplier who carries the Tattle Tale. Sounds good, and it comes with "adjustable sensitivity," a virtue it shares with many politicians. Like the Scat Mat, the Tattle Tale is a party animal, too. Put one in your medicine cabinet to embarrass snoopy guests.

The Snappy Trainer, about the size of a ping-pong paddle, " 'springs' and makes a loud snapping noise," startling an animal, "but not harming him," when he lands on it. Advertised as "a humane alternative to the mousetrap" for keeping animals off the furniture—which is like advertising a mugger as a humane alternative to a serial killer—the Snappy Trainer costs a mere $4.85 for a package of three. Once again, the pet owner will find countless ways to get extra enjoyment from the Snappy Trainer, especially if he or she uses it in conjunction with the Scat Mat.

The attentive reader has noticed, perhaps, a wry skepticism regarding some of these training aids, particularly the Scat Mat and the Snappy Trainer. Not all readers may share that skepticism. Indeed, some people may see nothing wrong with using three or four "harmless shocks" to keep Toby off the loveseat on which he loves to sit. Let your conscience and your adjustable sensitivity be your guides.

Estep reports that some cat owners use plastic carpet runners to discourage cats from jumping onto certain surfaces. "The bottoms of those runners have sharp, little points that dig into the carpet," he explains, "and if you place the runner pointy side up, you create a surface that most cats do not like to walk on. That can provide an aversive stimulus the cat will avoid."

Additional aversive stimuli can be provided by placing a cookie sheet filled with water on kitchen countertops you do not want your cat visiting or lining a windowsill with pencils to make it unsuitable for resting. Leave a ¼- to ⅜-inch gap (.6-cm–1.9-cm) between the pencils so they will roll when your cat lands on them. Carpets, countertops, or just about any surface can be lined with double-sided sticky tape to discourage your cat from walking or roosting there.

As these engaging portraits suggest, photographers are among the world's best cat trainers.

Like punishment, aversive stimuli alone may not be sufficient to discourage unwanted behavior. If you line a kitchen counter with sticky tape and leave an open can of cat food on it, your cat is liable to decide that the need for food is greater than the discomfort of taking a few steps on sticky tape. Therefore, the sticky tape will not be sufficient to deter him.

Chapter 8
Intermediate Training

In *The Cat and the Curmudgeon* Cleveland Amory observes that his feline housemate Polar Bear is a true conservative because he doesn't like anything to happen that has not happened before. Cats are, indeed, creatures of unvarying routine. They prefer to have the same significant events happen at the same times each day. They prefer certain resting places, certain toys, and, if they are indulged unwisely, they prefer a certain few foods to the exclusion of all others. This preference for a well-ordered life is somewhat surprising in an animal with a reputation for being a supreme individualist. Granted, cats may not find curiosity entirely killing, but they prefer to find it on their own and are largely discommoded when it finds them instead. Yet rather than being exasperated by a cat's single-mindedness, the perceptive owner will turn it to advantage when training a cat.

The PURR Method

Patience

Patience, understanding, reward, and repetition (PURR) are the keys to successful training. Because your patience will be alternately tried and rewarded while you are teaching Muffin to sit, stay, beg, and so on, do not begin training if the heel marks of a frustrating day are stamped across your brow. The last thing you need at that point is another frustration in the person of a recalcitrant cat who, purely out of spite and malice, of course, refuses to do what you ask.

In truth, Muffin does not refuse your petition out of spite or malevolence. Those are human qualities that human beings project onto

After each training session, tell your cat what a good job he did.

animals, especially when humans are keyed up because of something the boss, the clerk at the convenience store, the person in the next cubicle at work, the President, some editorial writer, a loved one, the neighbor's kid, or all of the above did or said recently. If your nose is out of joint, you should chop wood, go jogging, work out for half an hour on the heavy bag, or put on your favorite album and the headphones. Leave the cat training for another day. All you need from your cat when you are cross is her nonjudgmental company while you sit and stare into space, brooding over the unfairness of it all.

Nancy Kobert trains animals for television and public appearances.

Understanding

Although cats long have been considered exceedingly difficult if not impossible to train, they are, in reality, neither. They are not so transparently eager to please as are dogs, who always have depended on the ability to function within a social hierarchy in order to survive, a dependence that leads them to crave our approval. Cats, for their part, have depended on nothing beyond their own hunting abilities to survive from time immemorial. If animals could play musical instruments, dogs would audition for a place in the symphony while cats would seek careers as soloists. Yet cats do court us when it pleases them, and some it pleases quite often. Moreover, they will respond to our requests if we make it worth-

while for them to do so and if those requests evolve naturally out of a longstanding relationship.

In addition to understanding how a cat's wires are arranged, people should understand their own motives for wanting to train their cats. The incentive for basic training is straightforward: You will respect your cat's needs if your cat respects your furniture. But why do you want your cat to come when you call, stay when you command her to, jump through a hoop, or sit up and beg?

Unless you plan to take walks out of doors with Muffin and to allow her some off-lead time for exploring when you do, an ill-advised proposition at best, you will not need to summon her in order to prevent her getting lost or into mischief. Nor will you need to have her stay put on command when she is about to go chasing off after another cat or some other distraction. And you can be sure that jumping through a hoop, sitting up and begging, and walking a plank serve little purpose to a cat, beyond securing for it a morsel of food.

What, then, is your motivation? Is a well-trained cat an ego enhancer? A way of showing off for company? A foil for an authoritarian personality? One hopes not. The litmus test for cat breeding, slightly modified, applies equally well to cat training: If performance training does not add as much to Muffin's life as it does to yours, she is better left untrained. Nor should you train a cat if you would not be willing to trade places with her for your next training session.

Reward

You must not expect Muffin to come bounding every time you call—or to do anything else you ask—unless she anticipates getting a reward every time she does. And cats, you would do well to remember, spell "reward" *f-o-o-d.*

"Cats are very business oriented," says Nancy Kobert. "When a dog is working with you, so much of what he does is for the social interaction, because of the group structure that dogs have always lived in. Cats, however, especially the ones our domestic cats are descended from, are primarily solitary animals. So, communication isn't all that motivating to a cat. What is important is the end result—the reward. That's why we have to train our cats to respond to their names with food. You don't have to use food to get dogs to respond to their names."

Dogs, like humans, consider the sound of their names the world's sweetest music. But cats, says Kobert, "just don't need that. And they don't need it because they don't really have the social instinct that other animals have."

They do, however, have a taste for treats, and they are willing to respond with their appetites if not with their emotions. Plan your reinforcements accordingly.

Repetition

Because cats are naturally cautious when something happens that has not happened before, training periods should be constructed of familiar routines that build confidence in your cat. Therefore:

1. Keep training sessions brief: three to five minutes at a time, two or three times a day.
2. Conduct training sessions in the same location with the same unfailing patience each time. After your cat has mastered a trick, you can vary the setting to see if that learning is transferable. Only if you are training your cat to perform in public should you vary the training site every few days.
3. Reward your cat with praise in addition to treats when she

does well. If she associates performance with good feelings, she will be more likely to perform willingly.

4. Do not use your cat's name to scold her if she makes a mistake during training. In fact, do not scold your cat at all during training. When she makes a mistake, show her by voice and example what you want her to do.

5. Limit your cat to one teacher. Different folks have different strokes when it comes to interacting with cats. This might be fine sociologically, but it plays havoc with the training experience.

6. If your cat attempts to leave before a training session is over, bring her back quietly and try again. Do not call her by name when you are trying to coax her back to the training site, or she might never come again when she is called.

7. Do not let the session end unless you are ready to end it.

8. Have a carrier handy in case the doorbell rings and you have to go and answer it in the middle of a training session. Put your cat in the carrier before you answer the door, send the person away, and go back to your training session. Of course you will not have to bother answering the phone during a training session if you have an answering machine.

The more advanced the cat trick, the easier it is to teach if it is broken down into its component parts and presented one step at a time.

9. Let other members of the household know that you do not wish to be disturbed during a training session.

10. When your cat is not catching on to a lesson as quickly as you would like, ask yourself what you are doing wrong. Are you going too quickly? Are you handling your cat too abruptly? Has an impatient tone infiltrated your voice? Are you rewarding your cat as soon as she does the right thing? Is it time to take a step back and go over a routine your cat already knows for a few days in order to build up her confidence before coming back to the trick that is giving her trouble?

Tools of the Trade

Training a cat does not require a lot of fancy equipment or sequined costumes. A steady table about 3 feet (.9 m) high, covered with a non-slip rubber mat or carpet remnant, and a pocketful of food treats are all you need to get started.

Some trainers prefer to offer their cats food rewards on the end of a wooden dowel during training sessions. The dowel, roughly 6 to 8 inches (15.2–20.3 cm) long and 1/4 inch (.6 cm) in diameter, can save the trainer a few scratches if an overeager cat reaches out for her reward too enthusiastically. To prepare the dowel, sharpen it in a pencil sharpener, then file the point to a rounded tip with just enough of an edge to allow you to spear a dollop of food from a can.

The Name Game

The naming of cats, as T.S. Eliot observed, is not a diversion to be taken lightly. But you can make a game out of teaching your cat to respond to her name, especially if you make your cat's name synonymous with food.

Whether you name your cat or she arrives with a name but does not know what it is, you can teach her to respond to that name by rewarding her with praise and food every time she does. Suppose, for example, you have decided to name your cat Muffin. Put a few treats in your pocket and settle down near Muffin one fine morning a few hours after she has been fed or one fine afternoon a few hours before dinner. The treat can be a piece of dry or semimoist kibble or some other tidbit in which Muffin has exhibited extreme interest in the past. For best results, the treat should be something Muffin does not receive every day as part of her regular diet.

Pronounce Muffin's name clearly and with a certain high-pitched ascending gusto. If she looks in any direction but yours, do nothing. Wait a second or two and say her name again. Unless she is stone deaf, Muffin will eventually look toward you. When she does, say "good" and reward her with a piece of whatever it is you have in your pocket.

You have Muffin's attention now. Pet her a few times and tell her what a good girl she is. Do not, however, say something like "that's a good Muffin" or use her name while praising her. You want her to turn toward you when you say "Muffin," so praise her with generic terms of endearment until she begins to look away from you. As soon as she does, say her name again. You may have to say it once or twice or even three times, but if you put enough urgency into your tone, Muffin will eventually look at you. When she does, make with the food. Praise her a few seconds, and after she is looking elsewhere, say her name again.

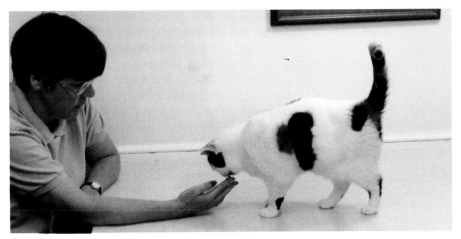

Cats can be trained to come when you call if there is something tasty in or on your hand.

After Muffin has responded to her name three or four times in one session, you have accomplished your mission. To build on your initial success, carry those tidbits around the house and break into a spontaneous name-training session several times a day.

Here, Kitty, Kitty

No team likes to lose the first game of the season. That is why many colleges choose first-game opponents that are better known for the size of their libraries than for the size of their athletes. Good starts build confidence, which builds success, which builds a winning season or a well-trained cat. Stumble in the first game and you will be playing catch-up when you attempt to teach your cat to sit, stay, lie down, roll over, jump through a hoop, or perform any of the more advanced tricks on the schedule.

"You should start with something that is easy for cats to do and to be rewarded for right away," says Kobert. "You want their first association with training to be fun, not difficult, confusing, or frustrating."

If you follow the example of most trainers, the first trick you will teach your cat is to come when she is called. Once your cat learns to respond to a vocal summons virtually without fail or insubordination, you will have established yourself as the nearest thing to a dominant animal in her life. You will have earned a measure of control over your cat, and you will be more confident when you teach your cat more complex tricks. That confidence will give your cat confidence in you, making her more comfortable about doing what you ask her to do.

Cats, as we have noted, are not prewired to answer readily any summons that does not involve food. (See Why Your Cat Does Not Come When You Call, page 43.) Instead of despairing over this tendency, design your first training sessions around it. In fact, that is what you did when you taught Muffin her name. If she is responding well to her name, teaching her to come when you call should not be difficult.

Many cats begin loitering in the kitchen well before mealtime. When they see the food bowl descending toward the floor, they zoom toward it instantly. You can make this tendency work to your advantage by saying "Muffin, come," before moving the bowl from the kitchen counter to the floor. (You could use "here" or any other word instead of "come" when you wish to summon Muffin, but once you have chosen a call word, use it exclusively.) It does not matter how old Muffin is when you begin this routine, but the best time to begin it is the first day you begin feeding her. (Of course, if you have not taught Muffin to respond to her name yet, you should say only "come" before you put the bowl of food on the floor.)

In addition to rewarding Muffin for coming when you call, be sure to add a lavish helping of praise before you set the bowl down. This will reinforce the behavior you desire because she will associate the word "come" with food and praise.

Some cats do not appear in the kitchen until they hear the rattle of the dry-food container, the sound of a can being opened, or the sound of the drawer where the can opener is kept being opened. If Muffin is one of those cats, say "Muffin, come" before doing any of these guaranteed-to-get-her-attention activities.

After two or three weeks you will have "trained" Muffin to come when you call. At mealtimes. But no doubt there will be other times of the day and other parts of the house where you will want her to answer this command readily.

Begin this second phase of training (it will be the first phase for those rare cats that do not race to the kitchen at the sound of the can opener) in a room from which there is no escape and no foolproof place for Muffin to hide. As you did when you trained Muffin to come when you called her to dinner, try to make this lesson fit into her normal routine. If, for example, Muffin likes to sit in the living-room window in the afternoon, you might wander into the living room with a few of Muffin's favorite treats in your pocket, close the door, and sit on the sofa. If Muffin begins to come over to greet you, say "Muffin, come" and take a treat out of your pocket. As soon as Muffin is close enough to get the treat, say "good" in a high-pitched, happy tone and reward her with the treat.

Some cat trainers recommend putting a touch of baby food on the end of a spoon, a dowel, or—if you wish—your finger. Hold the food a few feet in front of Muffin and say "Muffin, come." As soon as she does, say "good" and give her the food.

"The word 'good' serves as a bridging stimulus," says Kobert. "It functions as an IOU. Let's say I want a cat to sit, he sits, and I want to reward him for it. By the time I put my hand in my pouch, get the food out, and take the steps forward to hand it to him, he may have scratched his chin or done something else. How is he going to understand which of those behaviors was the one that got him the treat?

"If you teach him to associate a sound with the arrival of the food—the sound of the word 'good,' for example—then you're literally giving him an IOU at the point at which he did the behavior appropriately. When you say 'good,' you're saying 'hang on a minute, I'm going to give you something.' So after you say 'good,' the arbitrary things the cat may do while waiting for that food will not make him confused about what the actual reinforceable behavior was."

Should Muffin appear more interested in what she was doing before you came in than in coming over to greet you, move casually to a spot about two or three feet from her. Say "Muffin, come," then offer her the treat. If Muffin comes to you, say "good" and give her the treat. If she ignores you, reach over quietly, pick her up, move her to you, praise her with pats and a hug—but not with the word "good"—and give her the treat. Save "good" for those occasions when Muffin has done the required action.

Praising a cat that just has ignored you might seem unwise, but you would be even less wise to allow Muffin to ignore you when she pleases. By picking Muffin up and moving her to the place where you want her to be, you are teaching her that she is either going to come when she is called or you are going to see that she does.

If Muffin runs off, do not give chase immediately and do not repeat the "come" command. Walk casually to her instead, pick her up, carry her back to the place from which you first summoned her, and praise her for coming. Skip the treat this time, so that she does not think you are a complete pushover. And remember, do not praise her with the word "good" unless Muffin has done the behavior that was required of her. "Good" serves only to let her know that what she has just done is a rewardable action.

If Muffin has complied with the "come" command two or three times before refusing, this would be a good time to end the lesson. If she runs off the first time you call, retrieve her. Praise her for coming, give her a treat, and place her on the floor a foot or two away from you. Say "Muffin, come" and produce another treat. Unless she is feeling particularly stubborn, she will come for the treat. If she does, say "good" and give her the treat. Then end the lesson. If she is feeling particularly stubborn, pick her up, bring her back to the spot from where she was called, praise her for "obeying," but do not give her a treat. Then end the lesson.

Once Muffin appears to have mastered this command, do not give her a food reward every time she comes when you call. Feline nature being what it is, if she knows she can get a treat every time she comes when she is called, she may decide on occasion that it would be more rewarding to continue what she was doing, even if she was doing nothing, than to get that old predictable treat. But if she does not get a treat every time, she will not be certain that treats are always forthcoming. Thus, she will be more likely to answer every time because she always will be hoping, as the old joke goes, that tonight is the night.

Psychologists call this maybe-yes, maybe-no technique *intermittent reinforcement.* They caution, however, that the schedule of intermittent reinforcement must not be predictable itself. If you withhold the treat every third time you summon Muffin, she will soon glom on to that fact and begin timing her refusals to coincide with the empty hand. To be effective, intermittent reinforcement must be random. If your training sessions consist of four or five practices of the "come" command during three or four sessions a day,

withhold the treat the second time you call Muffin during the first session, the fourth time during the second session, and so on.

Do not be intermittent with your praise, however. You do not want Muffin thinking you do not like her if she does not respond at once. Nor do you want her to think that you love her any the less for some performances than for others. Every time she comes when you call, say "good," even if you do not give her a treat.

Repeat the "come" exercise a few times a day, limiting the distance Muffin has to travel to three or four feet and restricting each session to two or three minutes in which Muffin has answered your call three or four times. After Muffin is coming to you consistently when you call, increase the distance between you and her by gradual increments: first, to four or five feet for several days and then to six or seven feet for several days. Keep increasing the distance between you and her until she responds to your command from across the room.

Finally, if you want to impress yourself, call her from the next room. For obvious reasons, the best room for you to be in when you first attempt this feat is the kitchen. And the best thing to do right after you call her is to rattle a box of dry food. After she is bounding regularly into the kitchen in response to this stimulus, call her without shaking the box, and give her copious applause and a treat if she comes running. If she does not, call her again and rattle the box this time. When Muffin appears, praise her and give her a treat.

Once Muffin is racing to the kitchen in response to your voice alone, try calling her from other rooms in the house. If Muffin is an only child, use the dry-food box as an auxiliary training aid at first, then try summoning her by voice only. If you have other cats, the sound of the dry-food box might draw a crowd, which would be counterproductive.

If at any point Muffin does not respond to your vocal summons from another room, do not make an issue of it and do not repeat the command. Perhaps she did not hear you, and even if she did, the worst conclusion she will reach is that she can ignore you on occasion when you are not in the same room as she. Even in that event you will still be miles ahead of the game. Most cats figure they can ignore their owners from any distance any time they choose.

Unless you have visions of retiring on the money Muffin earns in the movies—or unless you have a fenced-in, escape-proof yard—you need not practice the "come" command anywhere but in your house. Some cat trainers suggest taking Muffin to a friend's house for a practice session, but asking a friend if you and Muffin can drop by to work on obedience training is

somewhat pushy. And if any of your friends should make the same request of you, say that your interior decorator is coming over that afternoon. (There is nothing wrong, however, with asking a friend to come over for a visit and then having Muffin stroll by for a show-and-tell at the same time.)

After you are pleased with Muffin's response to the "come" command, test her resolve, and yours, by adding some distractions to the routine. Call her while she is sitting in the living-room window watching traffic. Call her when she is playing with a toy or with another cat. If she responds, good for her and you. If she does not, you will have to pick her up, carry her to the spot from which you summoned her, and reward her with praise and a treat.

If your cat is colossally inflexible and refuses to come when you call—and if you are just as inflexible in your desire to teach her to respond to this command—put her harness on her and attach the six-foot training lead to it (see Walking on Lead, page 96). Then say, "Muffin, come" and tug gently and briefly on the lead. If she does not respond to the call-tug summons, call her again and tug on the lead. If there is still no answer, pick her up and carry her to the spot from which you summoned her. Praise her lavishly but do not give her a treat. Then dismiss the class. Until she begins answering to "Muffin, come" with no more prompting than a short tug on the lead, you must end every lesson by carrying her into base.

Eventually, Muffin should begin responding to the "come" command with little more than a gentle tug on the lead by way of spiritual guidance. This is your signal to eliminate the tug after you have called her. If she responds to your voice only, her reward should be prodigious. If she is not yet voice-activated, revert to tugging on the lead as a means of inspiring her to come when called.

When that glorious day on which Muffin comes to you in response to your voice alone finally dawns, bask in the glory of several more of those days. Then try the exercise without benefit of harness and lead. If Muffin ignores you, go back to the harness and lead—or accept graciously the fact that she may never come when she is called, a fact that is not going to change your life or hers significantly as long as she is not allowed off lead outdoors (where a situation in which she has to come when she is called for her own safety may arise).

From Muffin's point of view, there are few reasons for calling a cat who lives indoors, and all of those reasons involve food. Whenever you call Muffin, she should be happy you did. Never call her when you want to give her medication, stuff her into a carrier for a trip to the vet's, or do anything else that might cause her discomfort. If she associates a summons with an unpleasant consequence, she will begin ignoring all summonses.

Walking on Lead

The great outdoors is not so great for a cat's health, well-being, or longevity. Indeed, the more time a cat spends outdoors, the greater her chances of being injured in a

A morning stroll through the neighborhood will brighten the routine of any cat.

fight with another animal, getting squished by a car, catching feline leukemia from one of her sidekicks, picking up fleas, ticks, or worms, being harassed or victimized by human bullies, eating pesticides or lapping up antifreeze, getting her leg caught in a steel-jaw trap, or coming to grief in any number of painful ways.

Nevertheless, cats love to go outside, and once they have stretched out on the picnic table for a midsummer afternoon's nap, chased a downpour of falling leaves in the autumn, sharpened their claws on a hundred-year-old tree, caught a mouse in the garage, or sampled any of the great outdoors' many delights, their owners are hard pressed to open and close a door quickly enough to keep a cat from scampering outside. But what a cat does not know, cannot hurt her. Therefore, if you acquire a cat while she is still a young, untraveled kitten, before she has learned that if she shows up at certain neighborhood doors at certain times she can expect a treat, make sure that her feet never touch anything but hardwood, carpet, linoleum, well-stuffed chairs, comfortable beds, and your veterinarian's examination table. Keep your cat inside where it is always summertime and the living is always easy and safe.

If you acquire a cat that is used to going outdoors, you can satisfy her keenness for fresh air by taking her for walks. Moreover, training your cat to a harness or collar and lead may prove helpful when you are trying to train the cat in other ways (see Here, Kitty, Kitty, page 91) because lead training establishes your control over your cat.

Although the idea of being demonstrably under someone else's control is foreign to the way a cat views the world, some cats are comfortable walking on lead from Step One. Others react to a harness or collar as if it were a straight jacket. They roll about distractedly, look at you as though you were a fiend, and refuse to take a step no matter how much you encourage or bribe them to do so. Indeed, some cats—whether from shyness or obstinacy—will never consent to walk on lead for more than a step or grudging two at a time. The majority of cats, however, will eventually concede if they think concession is to their benefit. And some cats even get to like the idea.

Most trainers prefer harnesses for lead training because they are virtually escapeproof, while collars are not. What's more, a collar might chafe Muffin's neck if she pulls against it in an effort to escape, and there is no point in adding discomfort to disorientation when you are trying to teach her to walk on a lead. Finally, many cats freeze when pressure is applied to their necks. If a cat is reluctant to walk on a lead, she is going to become more reluctant if you are pulling on her neck to encourage her to move.

The only time you should consider using a cat collar to train your cat to walk on a lead is if she goes thoroughly catatonic over the harness. In that situation, use an adjustable, nonslip collar. Choke chains, sometimes euphemistically called *check* chains, are unnecessary for controlling a cat; and breakaway collars are better suited for everyday use, where their breakaway capacity could prevent Muffin from hanging herself while climbing or playing. You do not, however, want her breaking away from you on the sidewalk.

A collar should not be so tight that it interferes with a cat's breathing. Nor should it be so loose that it slips over a cat's ears when she has decided she has had enough of lead training and puts herself into reverse.

Cat harnesses made of nylon or felt-backed leather are available at pet shops and from suppliers that advertise in cat magazines. No mat-

Many cats break out into a break dance at the sight of the harness and lead.

ter what the material, a harness should be adjustable; and when it is placed on a cat, it should be fitted snugly enough so that the cat cannot wriggle out of it, yet not so snugly as to be uncomfortable.

A lead should be lightweight and well constructed. The material of which it is constructed is secondary. Leather, nylon, or cotton are all suitable (chain is really a bit much) as long as the lead and the snap on the end of the lead are securely attached. And the snap should close securely enough so that it will remain attached to the harness if your cat tries to bolt.

Leads also are available at pet shops and from suppliers that advertise in cat magazines. Although leads come in different lengths, a six-foot lead not only will keep your cat from running off but also will teach her to stay by your side while the two of you are out walking. If you are inclined to give your cat a little more room outdoors, buy a ten-foot lead instead. You can shorten it if necessary by wrapping it around your hand a few times when you want your cat close to you.

Lead training, like charity, begins in the home. Kittens as young as 10 to 12 weeks of age can be acclimated to a harness, but you probably will not want to take a cat that young for a walk, especially if she has not had all her shots. Introduction to a harness can wait until a kitten is a little older and is ready to begin going for walks

outside. If you acquire an adult cat, wait until she is used to her new surroundings before acquainting her with a harness.

Some trainers suggest a brisk, straight-ahead introduction: Put the harness on the cat gently and let her wear it for a few minutes. Other trainers suggest placing the harness where your cat is going to see it—a favorite resting place around the house or, better yet, the table on which you groom your cat—and giving the cat a few days or a week to get used to the sight and scent of this device. All trainers caution against letting any reluctance that a cat might have to wearing a harness escalate into a face-off, namely yours.

Whether you prefer the straight-away or the gradual-introduction method, the installation of the harness should be preceded by a moment or two of stroking, unctuous praise, and a few treats. When your cat is purring away blissfully, position her so that she is facing away from you and place the harness over her back. Here again, trainers are of two minds regarding procedure. One mind says to attach the harness, the other says to let it lie on your cat's back a few seconds a day for several days before trying to attach it fully. The method you choose will depend on your cat's reaction to the harness. If she does not seem to mind it, you might as well hook it up and be done with it. Be sure to give your cat a treat once the harness is in place.

If your cat recoils in horror at the harness, pat her a few seconds if you can, remove the harness tenderly, and try again tomorrow. (If you opted for the straight-ahead method and your cat reacts poorly to the harness, perhaps you should allow her to see it around the house and at grooming time for a few days or a week before you try to install it again.)

After your cat consents to wearing the harness—which consent may be accompanied by a period of rolling, scratching, and complaining—leave the harness on for 5 or 10 minutes a day, for several days. Then leave it on for 10 or 15 minutes a day, and, finally, for 15 to 20 minutes a day after that.

The lead should be added to the harness in much the same way the harness was added to the cat—gradually. The first time you put the lead on Muffin, allow her to drag it around for five minutes or so and give her one or two treats during that interlude, then remove the lead. Repeat this routine for two or three days.

Once Muffin is comfortable with the lead, pick up one end of it and hold it. Do not try to lead her anywhere, simply hold the lead while she moves about, following after her wherever she goes. Remove the lead after three or four minutes.

Now you are ready to have Muffin follow where you lead. To accomplish this, Muffin should be on your left, your left arm should be held naturally by your side, and the lead should be in your left hand. Turn your body toward Muffin, show her the treat you have in your right hand, and take a step or two forward. If she steps toward the food, move a few additional steps forward. If she steps forward again, give her the treat. If she is reluctant to move, do not drag her. Move the food a little closer. As soon as she moves toward it, say "good," give her the food, and praise her for moving. If she refuses to move, pick her up, carry her forward to the place from which you called her, praise her for being a wonderful cat, but do not give her the treat. Then end the lesson for the day.

Consider it a moral victory if Muffin moves a few steps the first day. On subsequent days, increase the distance she must walk alongside you before she gets her treat. Before long she will be walking all around the house.

When you decide to take your cat-walking act on the road, begin in your own driveway or back yard. And do not be discouraged if Muffin freezes up and does not move. In that event, sit quietly beside her, reassuring her that the big, old world is not as cruel as it looks. That should reassure her, even if it is only half true. Then give her a treat and take her back indoors. The next time you venture outside—or the time after that—she will probably begin to walk along beside you. If she does not, do not

make a federal case out of it. Perhaps she has acquired an ability that one philosopher believed would make the world a better place: the ability to stay quietly in one's room.

If Muffin decides she wants to see more of the world, the radius of that world will equal the length of her lead. She may eventually test that radius. If she does, do not drag her back to you. Simply stop, hold the lead firmly, and wait for Muffin to move in your direction, then continue walking. She will be more inclined to move in your direction if a treat magically appears in your right hand. If Muffin tries to train you by refusing to move in hopes that you will give her another treat, pick her up and carry her for a while. Then put her down and continue walking.

Sit

After Muffin responds to the sound of her name and walks cheerfully on a lead, she is ready to advance to her next assignment—sitting on command. Select a quiet, well-confined place to begin training, one that is free from the distractions presented by other animals or other humans. The time to present a trick before an audience is after a cat has learned that trick, not while the cat is learning it.

A table about 3 feet (.9 m) high, covered with a nonslip rubber mat or carpet remnant and located in a corner of a room with the door closed, constitutes a proper setting. This arrangement provides you with a comfortable working space and the cat with few avenues of escape. The table, if it is high enough, also allows you to sit down and make yourself comfortable while you are working with her.

Before long Muffin will associate the training setting with tricks and the treats that follow them and, if training sessions are pleasant and rewarding, will put on her game face when taken to the training room. To avoid confusing her—and making grooming sessions somewhat difficult—do not train her on the same table on which she is groomed. Otherwise, she might be looking for treats all the time she is being combed or brushed.

Begin teaching the "sit" command by placing Muffin a few feet away from you on the table and giving the "come" command. This will get her attention and will establish a cooperative spirit of goodwill on

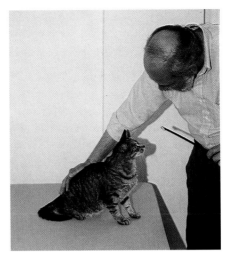

To teach your cat to sit, begin by giving the "sit" command, then exert a gentle, downward pressure on the cat's rump.

which to build the "sit" lesson. After Muffin has consumed a treat for coming promptly on command, pick her up, place her 12 to 18 inches (30–46 cm) in front of you, face toward yours, and run one hand gently down her spine. If she is like most other cats, she will arch her back in pleasure about the time you reach her tail. When she does, say "sit" and exert a slight but authoritative downward pressure on her rump. If Muffin deigns to sit

The "Sit" Command

1. Place your cat on the training table 12 to 18 inches (30–46 cm) in front of you, face toward yours.
2. Run one hand gently down her spine.
3. When you reach the base of her tail, say "sit" and exert a slight downward pressure on her rump.
4. If your cat sits, say "good," and after she has been sitting still for a few seconds, give her a food reward.
5. If she refuses to sit, repeat steps 2 and 3 until she does, then proceed to Step 4.

down, say "good," and after she has been sitting still for a few seconds, give her a treat.

Although you used her name when you taught Muffin the "come" command, you should not use her name when you are teaching her the "sit" command. By now Muffin associates her name with a request to move toward you. She might think that is what you want her to do when you say her name before telling her to sit. Saying "Muffin, sit" or "Muffin, stay" may be more confusing than the simple "sit" or "stay" command.

If Muffin refuses to move when you exert the slight but authoritative downward pressure on her rump, take a deep breath and take your hand off her rump. Do not repeat the "sit" command. You do not want her to think she has the option

Cats are fond of sitting pretty, a tendency the adroit trainer will turn to his or her advantage.

of obeying a command on the second, third, or tenth request.

Go back, instead, to the run-your-hand-gently-down-her-spine step and say "sit" when you get to her rump. Increase the pressure a tad on her rump if you want, but do not increase it to any extent that might be considered punitive. If she still does not get the message, run your hand down her spine once more and try the "sit" command again.

If three minutes go by and Muffin is still standing there looking at you with confusion or disdain, take one of her hind legs in each of your hands and set her down gently in the sitting position while saying "sit." Having thus walked her through the lesson, praise her lavishly for "obeying" and end the exercise. Do not give her a treat. It is fine for her to know you still love her even though she has not completed the task without assistance, but you do not want her to think she deserves a treat simply for outwaiting you. Love is unconditional. Rewards are not. That is why rewards are more effective in manipulating animals and people.

Eventually, after you have returned to the "sit" exercise a sufficient number of times over a sufficient number of days, Muffin will begin sitting in response to the pressure of your hand on her rump. When that happens, lighten up on the pressure until she begins sitting in response to your voice alone. After she has stayed in the sitting position for two or three seconds, give her praise and a treat, then lift her up into a standing position before telling her to sit again.

Once Muffin has learned the "sit" command on the table, vary the routine by trying the command on a chair seat and after that on the floor. Otherwise, she may get the idea that the only time she must obey you is when the two of you see eye to eye. And after she obeys the command as readily on the floor as she did on the table and the chair, begin lengthening the distance from which you give the command until she is obeying you from 10 or 15 feet away. Reinforce obedience with praise and, intermittently, with treats. Do not allow Muffin to come to you for the treat. Take the treat to her.

While you are teaching Muffin to sit, you also will need to teach her when it is all right to stop sitting. That word or signal is called the release. Some trainers use a verbal release such as "all done" or "all right," which they use at the same time they are lifting Muffin into a standing position. If you choose a verbal release, make sure it is not the same one you use when praising Muffin.

A few trainers prefer a signal rather than a word release. Thus, you might release Muffin from a "sit" by clapping your hands, snapping your fingers, waving one hand toward you beckoningly, or some other motion that inspires her to stand up.

The trainee looks alert, and the trainer looks like a traffic cop in this illustration of the "stay" command in the down position.

Stay

Once Muffin is sitting pretty, she is ready for the "stay" command. Indeed, there is little benefit in teaching her to sit if she will not remain seated long. Therefore, it is time to teach Muffin that "stay" simply means "sit longer."

After doing a few preliminary sits, instead of releasing Muffin from the last one, hold your right hand, palm toward Muffin, in front of her face as if she were oncoming traffic and you were a police officer. Then say "stay." If she attempts to get up, push her back into the sitting position with your left hand and repeat the "stay" command.

After she holds the sitting position for a few seconds, praise her and give her a treat, then release her. Pat her a few seconds then tell her to sit.

The "Stay" Command

1. Place your cat in the "sit" position.
2. Hold your right hand, palm toward your cat, in front of her face.
3. Say "stay."
4. If your cat holds the sitting position for a few seconds, say "good" and give her a treat.
5. If she attempts to get up, guide her back into the sitting position with your left hand and repeat the "stay" command.

Then tell her to stay again. If she does, give her a treat and end the lesson. If she does not, push her into a sitting position and give the command. Hold her in position if you have to, praise her, end the lesson, but do not give her a treat.

As you practice "stay" on subsequent days, Muffin should begin to hold her position longer and longer until she is staying for 10, 15, or 20 seconds. As you increase the amount of time Muffin will stay seated, increase the distance between you and her. Instead of standing with your right hand a short distance in front of her face, move back until you are facing her from a distance of one foot. If she stays for you then, increase the distance gradually until you are five to ten feet away from Muffin and she is sitting like a regal statue.

Control your enthusiasm during this wait. If you smile broadly or praise her verbally, Muffin is liable to misinterpret that as a summons or a release. Without looking threatening, you should use a blank or serious expression while Muffin is on hold.

After Muffin has held her ground the length of time you require, say "good," walk quietly back to the table, and give her a treat. (You can introduce variation into the lesson by practicing the "sit" and "stay" commands every few days on the floor instead of on the table.)

As you increase the distance between you and Muffin while she is responding to "stay," she may stand up or even jump down from the table. If she does, retrieve her quietly, put her back on the table, and begin again.

If you want to test Muffin's mastery of the "stay" command, place her on the table and, while she is standing there, say "stay." If she holds her standing position, both of you have done a fine job. If she does not, you now have another variation of "stay" on which to work.

Chapter 9
Advanced Training

Lie Down

Although you will begin to teach your cat to lie down while he is in a sitting position, the ultimate goal is to have him perform this trick after you have given him the "lie down" command while he is standing up. If Toby has mastered the "sit" command (see page 100), he probably will sit down if you run your hand down his spine toward his tail and exert a gentle pressure on his rump without saying anything to him because this is how he first was taught to sit. Therefore, begin teaching the "down" command by placing Toby on his training table, telling him how wonderful he is, and guiding him gently into the sitting position. Do not give him the "sit" command because you do not want him to confuse that command with the "lie down" command which is the object of this lesson. You have to finesse him into sitting without telling him so.

Once Toby is sitting comfortably, give him a treat without telling him "good" before you do. Remember to save "good" for reinforcing the behavior that is being taught in a

lesson. Next, place one hand or the dowel on Toby's shoulders and the other hand behind his front legs a little above his ankles. Say "down," and as soon as you do, slide Toby's front legs toward you while using the hand that is on his shoulders to keep him from standing up or trying to escape.

As soon as you have guided Toby into the down position, say "good" and give him a treat, making sure that he stays in the down position. You may have to keep your hand on his shoulder to accomplish this. After Toby has held the down position for two or three seconds, release him by

Training is often a hands-on process. This cat, having achieved the "down" position, is being encouraged to hold that pose.

saying "okay" or whatever word you have settled on to release him from a trick (see page 103).

Praise Toby lavishly at this point. While you are doing so, guide him into a sitting position without telling him to sit, and practice the "down" command again. As you have done when teaching other commands to Toby, make sure he completes the routine at least once before you end the training session, and make sure he completes the routine the last time you ask him to before you end the session—even if you have to place him in the desired position.

You may have to guide Toby into the down position for several training sessions before he finally begins to extend his front legs into that position in response to your vocal command only. When he does, take your hand off his shoulders. If he starts to get up, say "stay" and put your hand back on his shoulders. Once he resumes the down position and stays there for a second or two, say "good" and give him a reward.

When Toby lies down consistently in response to your "down" command and remains in that position without the aid of your restraining hand for a few seconds, he has mastered the first half of the command. To teach him the second half, simply give him the command while he is standing up. If he is exceptionally responsive and you are exceptionally good at training, he will lie down at once. Chances

are he will look at you quizzically instead. In that case, put one hand on his rump to guide him into the sitting position, then place that hand on his shoulders while you guide his front legs into the down position. As soon as he gets into that position, which should be familiar to him by now, give him a reward. (But do not say "good" before you do.)

Release Toby from the down position, give him a few pats and kisses, take a deep breath, and give him the "down" command again. If he does not respond, guide him into the position as you did before. After he has held the position for two or three seconds, give him a reward.

Unless Toby is particularly thick, eventually he will lie down from a standing position. If he seems unable to grasp this idea, lying down from a sitting position may be the best you will be able to teach him to do. In that event, you can link the "sit" and "down" commands. Tell Toby to sit, but say nothing when he does. While he is sitting, give him the "down" command. When he lies down, say "good" and give him his reward. To keep Toby from anticipating the "down" command whenever you tell him to sit— and to keep him from sitting and then lying down immediately when you say "sit"—vary the routine by giving the "sit" command and then saying "good" as soon as Toby sits. Because he knows that "good"

Lie Down

1. Guide your cat into a sitting position.
2. Place one hand on your cat's shoulders and the other hand behind his front legs a little above his ankles.
3. Say "down" and as soon as you do, slide your cat's front legs toward you with one hand while using the hand that is on his shoulders to keep him from standing up or trying to escape.
4. As soon as you have guided your cat into the down position, say "good" and give him a treat, making sure that he stays in the down position. You may have to keep your hand on his shoulder to accomplish this.
5. After your cat has held the down position for two or three seconds, release him by saying "okay" or whatever word you have settled on to release him from a trick (see page 103).
6. Repeat this sequence until your cat is lying down without any assistance from you.

means he is going to get a treat soon, he should hold the sitting position while waiting for his reward. If he does, treat him and release him without going into the "down" command. If he begins to lie down before you treat him, place him in a standing position and try the "sit" command again.

Once Toby is lying down on command, whether from a sitting or a standing position, add the "stay" command (see page 103) to the routine after you have rewarded Toby for responding promptly to "down." Instead of releasing him from the down position after you have given him his treat, say "stay" and take a step or two back. Count to three. If Toby remains down, say "good" and give him a treat. You can gradually increase the distance between you and Toby if you like. If he begins to get up after you have told him to stay and have taken a step or

Beggars can be choosers if they play their tricks right.

two back from the table, walk over to him, put him in the down position, and give him the "stay" command again. Only this time do not move back. Save that for another day's lesson.

After Toby has learned to lie down on the table, you can teach him to do the same on the floor. Varying the location of the lesson keeps Toby from getting bored and provides you with a way to measure your success as a cat trainer.

Sit Up and Beg

The Table Method

Place Toby gently on his training table, which always should be covered with a smooth, nonslip rubber material or carpet remnant. Give him a few pats and tell him what a good boy he is. Then, facing him from a short distance in front of the table, hold your dowel (see Tools of the Trade, page 90), properly loaded with a dollop of food, a few inches above his head. Do not wave the dowel or touch him with it because that probably will inspire him to strike at the dowel in annoyance, and that is not the reaction you want. What you want him to do is to reach out with one or both paws to grasp the tip of the dowel. At that point, say "beg" and slowly raise the dowel up and away from you a few inches. As he continues to reach for the food, he will eventually attain the desired sit-up-and-beg position.

Once Toby has attained that position and held it for two or three seconds, say "good" and reward him with a treat from your pocket and with lavish praise. Be sure to say "good" and to offer the treat while Toby is still in the sit-up-and-beg position because you want to establish a connection between performing this trick and receiving an immediate reward. If you are slow with the treat, Toby may return to all fours. Should that happen at any time before he has attained and held the desired position, do not treat him. Go back to step one instead and begin the routine again.

If you use a treat from your pocket to reward Toby instead of letting him have the food on the dowel, you will not have to reload the dowel each time you practice this trick. In addition, eventually you will be able to do the trick in public using the empty dowel (or an upward wave of your arm) to coax Toby into sitting up properly.

Once Toby is sitting up properly, move the dowel toward you a few inches before you say "good" and give him his reward. This will increase the length of time that Toby can hold the sit-up position.

During subsequent sit-up-and-beg lessons, do not give Toby a treat every time he performs this trick successfully. If he does the trick four times during a session, for example, reward him for only two of those performances. One of those rewards should be for the final

Sit up and Beg

1. Place your cat on the training table.
2. Facing him from a short distance in front of the table, hold your dowel (see Tools of the Trade, page 90), properly loaded with a dollop of food, a few inches above his head.
3. When your cat reaches out with one or both paws to grasp the tip of the dowel, say "beg" and slowly raise the dowel up and away from you a few inches. As he continues to reach for the food, he will eventually attain the desired sit-up-and-beg position.
4. Once your cat has attained that position and held it for two or three seconds, say "good" and reward him with a treat from your pocket and with lavish praise.

performance so that the lesson ends pleasantly for him.

As Toby becomes more competent at sitting up, gradually begin to increase the length of time he has to sit up before receiving his reward. Depending on his willingness and balance—and your patience—he eventually should be able to sit between five and ten seconds before receiving a treat.

Because you have been saying "beg" faithfully each time you guided your cat into the sit-up-and-beg position with the help of your dowel, he well might respond to your voice command alone, especially if you accompany that command with a slight upward motion of your arm. If he does respond, let him know how pleased you are by the tone of your voice when you say "good" and the generosity of his reward. Many cats, however, will not sit up and beg without a certain amount of prompting from the ever-present dowel.

The Floor Method

You also can teach Toby to beg by holding food in your hand slightly out of reach above his head. (Some cats are rather enthusiastic about reaching for food held anywhere near their faces. If your cat is one of these and you wish to protect your fingers, use your dowel instead, properly loaded with a dollop of food.) Unless you are using thoroughly unappetizing food as bait for this trick, Toby will stand on his hind legs while reaching for the treat with his front paws. (Be sure his claws are freshly trimmed before trying this method.)

Say "beg" as you hold the treat above Toby's head. At the same time guide him gently into the desired position with your other hand if necessary. Be sure to hold the treat high enough so that he has to reach for it. If you hold the food too low, he is apt to stretch out one paw to grab it. Do not give him the treat until he has attained and held the proper position for two or three seconds. Otherwise he will think that "beg" simply means to stand on his hind legs and dance around appealingly. After Toby has begun begging smartly on command, begin intermittent reinforcement to cement his good behavior.

No matter which method you use to teach Toby to sit up and beg, the "stay" command is helpful for holding him in position if he begins to wobble or to show signs of wanting to return to all fours after he has been sitting up for only a second or two.

Cats that learn to beg may do so spontaneously in hopes of receiving food from other members of the family or from house guests. If you have no objection to this waifish behavior, fine. If you do object, be sure to let other people know they are never—under pain of excommunication—to reward your cat for impromptu begging demonstrations.

Shake Hands

Not long after humans had begun shaking hands with one another, some enterprising individual no doubt got the idea to extend a hand to animals as well. Thus was born one of the most elementary, popular, and easy-to-teach tricks in the well-behaved cat's repertoire.

Begin by placing your cat on his training table and giving him the "sit" command. Follow this with the "stay" command. Then extend your hand as though you were going to shake hands with your cat. At the same time, nudge your cat with your other hand right behind the elbow of the leg you want him to raise. The nudge should be gentle, but hardy enough to inspire your cat to lift that leg. As you nudge him, say "shake."

If he raises his paw on cue, say "good" and give him a treat. If he does not raise the desired leg, nudge him again while saying "shake." As soon as he consents to raise his leg the slightest distance off the table—or even to move it—take his leg gratefully in your hand, being careful not to wring it too heartily in your excitement, then say "good" and reward your cat.

Do not ask Toby to shake hands more than three or four times without success. If he is not in the mood that day, simply reach out, take hold of his leg, and lift it off the table. Then give him a treat, but do not say "good" before you do, just as if he had done the trick correctly on the first request. (Remember, "good" is a bridging stimulus used to let your cat know that the behavior he just exhibited was the desired one and that it is the behavior he is going to be rewarded for doing.)

In subsequent lessons, after your cat has begun to respond reliably to the gentle prompt of a nudge behind the elbow, ask him to shake hands, but do not touch his leg. If he does not extend a paw, nudge him with your free hand and reward him as soon as he raises his leg. Later in that lesson or early in the next one, see if he will shake hands in response to your voice command alone, for that is the goal you want to achieve. People will not be impressed overmuch if your cat will shake hands only after being prodded into doing so. As you have done with other tricks, reward your cat randomly once he has begun responding suitably to your voice commands.

Persons with enormous patience —or an inordinate desire to have the best-behaved cat on the block—may want to try to make

Shortly after humans began shaking hands with each other, they began shaking hands with their cats.

their cats ambidextrous in shaking hands. Once your cat has become handy at this trick—extending, say, his left front paw into your right hand every time you say "shake"— place your left hand close to his right front paw and see if he will give you that paw instead. If he does, you can make it seem as if he understands the difference between left and right if you say, "shake left" when asking for his left paw or "shake right" when asking for his right one.

Shake Hands

1. Place your cat on his training table and give him the "sit" command.
2. Then give him the "stay" command.
3. Extend your hand as though you were going to shake hands with your cat.
4. At the same time, nudge your cat with your other hand right behind the elbow of the leg you want him to raise.
5. As you nudge him, say "shake."
6. If he raises his paw on cue, say "good" and give him a treat.
7. If he does not raise the desired leg, nudge him again while saying "shake." As soon as he consents to raise his leg the slightest distance off the table—or even to move it— take his leg gratefully in your hand, say "good" and reward your cat.

Roll Over

1. Sit or kneel in front of your cat on the floor and put him in the down position. (If he knows the "down" command, use it to get him into the correct position. If not, show him where you want him to be by placing him in the down position with your hands.)
2. Hold one hand across your cat's paws so that he cannot move them.
3. With your other hand hold a treat a few inches directly above a point midway between your cat's eyes.

When he looks up to see what you have for him, say "roll" and begin moving your hand slowly in a circular motion so that the treat moves above one eye and toward his shoulder. As soon as your cat begins to swivel his head in the direction of the treat, say "good" and let him have the treat.

4. Repeat this several times and end the lesson.
5. Move the treat a little farther on each successive day you practice this trick until your cat is rolling over.

An alternative way to teach your cat to shake hands is by using a wide piece of doweling to which you have attached a Ping-Pong ball or a small rubber ball. If you use this method, says Nancy Kobert, "dip the ball into a can of good-tasting cat food, hold the ball in front of your cat, and say 'shake.' As soon as he reaches out and touches the ball, say 'good' and reward him. Be sure to say 'good' and to present the reward at the exact moment the cat touches the ball with his paw—before he grabs the ball with his claws and tries to pull it back to his face.

"You want to capture the behavior at the point when the cat's foot touches the ball, not when he touches and pulls, because you don't want to reinforce him for pulling the ball toward his face. That's reinforcing prey behavior, and you don't want to do that because you don't want to get scratched when you reward the cat or when you start doing the trick without the dowel. What you want to do is make the cat reach out and touch the ball. As soon as that paw contacts the ball, say, 'good' and feed the cat.

"This is the same technique they use to get Shamu to jump out of the water at Sea World. They touch the target on Shamu's nose and reward him. They touch it on his nose again and reward him. Then they'll hold the target an inch away.

Shamu knows that touching that target is reinforcing, so he comes forward and bumps it. Eventually he's jumping three stories out of the water."

Roll Over

Rolling over is not the most comfortable trick for a cat to perform because it violates his instinct for self-control. Moreover, because your cat could get hurt if he rolled off the training table, this trick should be taught only on the floor.

Sit or kneel in front of Toby and put him in the down position. If he knows the "down" command, use it to get him into the correct position. If not, show him where you want him to be by placing him in the down position with your hands.

Hold one hand across Toby's paws so that he cannot move them. With your other hand hold a treat a few inches directly above a point midway between his eyes. When he looks up to see what you have for him, say "roll" and begin moving your hand slowly in a circular motion so that the treat moves above one eye and toward his shoulder. As soon as Toby begins to swivel his head in the direction of the treat, say "good" and let him have the treat. Repeat this several times and end the lesson.

Move the treat a little farther on each successive day you practice this trick. Eventually you will pass

the point of no return, the point at which Toby can no longer follow the progress of the treat as you pass it over his shoulder and above his back. At that juncture, remove your hand from over his paws. He will have to roll over in order to follow the treat. When he does, say "good" and give him his reward.

After Toby is rolling over in one direction, either clockwise or counterclockwise, practice rolling over in the opposite direction to keep the routine from getting stale. After he is rolling over ambidextrously, try standing up when you ask him to perform this trick.

Teaching a cat to roll over takes several lessons. This cat is about half way through the training course.

Jump Through a Hoop

This is one of the easier tricks to teach a cat—especially if a cat is hungry. If the training table you have been using with Toby is not big enough for him to leap through a hoop on it without being in danger of falling off, you can teach this trick on the floor. We will assume for purposes of illustration, however, that the table is large enough for jumping.

Put a plate of food on one end of the table. Put Toby on the other end. Put a hoop on the table between Toby and the food and say "jump." Unless Toby is totally uninterested in eating and/or is totally freaked out by the hoop, he will step through the hoop eventually to get to the food. When he does, say "good," give him a reward out of your pocket, let him have a bite or two of the food on the plate, then move the plate to the other end of the table.

If he refuses to walk through the hoop, pick him up with one hand and guide him through it. Give him a treat, but do not say "good" and do not let him have any of the food on the plate.

If Toby walks through the hoop once and decides that the food on the plate was worth the effort, he will walk through the hoop again as soon as you say "jump" in order to get to the plate. If he does, say "good," give him a reward, and let him nibble a bit from the plate, too. Move the plate one more time and give him the "jump" command again. After he walks through the hoop to get to the food a third time, say "good," give him a treat, and let him take a few bites from the plate.

Jump Through a Hoop

1. Place your cat on the training table. If the table is not large enough for jumping, teach this trick on the floor.
2. Put a plate of food on one end of the table.
3. Put your cat on the other end.
4. Put a hoop on the table between your cat and the food and say "jump."
5. When your cat steps through the hoop, say "good," give him a reward out of your pocket, and let him have a bite or two of the food on the plate.
6. Move the plate to the other end of the table and repeat steps 4 and 5.
7. Raise the hoop about an inch (2.5 cm) off the table and repeat steps 4 and 5.
8. On subsequent days, keep raising the hoop gradually until your cat is jumping through it.

Then praise him generously, and end the training session for the day.

The next day—or the day following whatever day Toby saunters through the hoop without hesitation—hold the hoop so that its bottom is an inch (2.5 cm) above the table and Toby has to step through the hoop to get to his food. When he does, say "good," reward him, and let him nibble a bit from the plate. Raise the hoop an inch on subsequent days until Toby is leaping through it in order to get his treat and the food on the plate.

Once Toby is jumping 9 inches (22.9 cm) through the hoop, begin intermittent reinforcement by not allowing him to eat from the plate after he gets his treat for jumping through the hoop. Finally, to test his commitment to hoop-jumping, omit the plate of food entirely and give him only the word "good" and the treat for jumping through the hoop.

You may have to show him the treat first when you ask him to jump through the hoop, but once you have weaned him away from the plate of food and he is jumping through the hoop for the treat alone, he probably will jump through the hoop even if he cannot see the treat.

While the cat in the top photo studies an ancient text on training and the cat lower right lies down on the job, the little, striped contestant wonders if this hoop is for jumping, too.

Chapter 10

The Healthy Cat

Cats that are unwell often misbehave or fail to perform their favorite tricks when you ask them. If your cat begins to eliminate outside the litter pan or if she is cross and grumpy or listless and indifferent when you ask her to sit up for her favorite treat, she may not be feeling her best.

Vital Signs

Like healthy kittens, healthy cats reflect their well-being in the way they look, behave, and tend to themselves. Healthy cats have bright eyes and cool, slightly damp noses. Their gums are neither pale nor inflamed. Their ears are free of dirt and wax. Their bodies are fit and well muscled, not paunchy or obviously thin. Their coats are immaculately groomed, without bald patches, scabs, or flea dirt. The area below their tails is free of dried waste or discolored fur.

Though they spend prodigious amounts of time in sleep, as many as 14 to 18 hours a day, healthy cats are otherwise active and alert. They display affection for their owners, concern for their appearance, and a keen interest in life and mealtimes. They are, in short, the cat's meow.

Trouble Signs

Perhaps the first suggestion that a cat is unwell is a lack of interest in food. One missed meal or a faint, desultory pass at the plate is not cause for apprehension, but the cat that misses two consecutive meals probably would benefit from a trip to a veterinarian—especially if its temperature is elevated or if it displays other symptoms of illness.

Indeed, some signs of illness are significant enough to warrant an immediate trip to the vet, as soon as you have called to describe the

Although cats like to investigate a dog's bowl, cats should have their own bowls and their own food. Dog food does not contain enough protein for a cat's needs.

difficulty and to say that you are on your way over. The following list details some of those emergency symptoms. Do not consider the list exhaustive and do not use it as a diagnostic tool. Think of it instead as a sailor's map, showing where other navigators have encountered reefs, shoals, and deep channels on voyages with their cats.

Take your cat to the vet at once if your pet:

- has a deep wound or one that is still bleeding after pressure has been applied to it
- seems drowsy after eating a foreign substance
- stops breathing after chewing on a plant
- has a temperature above 105°F (40.6°C)
- exhibits a sudden weakness in the hindquarters that makes it difficult to walk
- has a red, ulcerated sore on its lips or any other part of its body
- develops an abscess that is warm and painful to the touch
- has a runny nose accompanied by a temperature above 103.5°F (39.5°C), pale gums, or weakness
- shows any evidence of trauma accompanied by shortness of breath, a temperature of 103.5°F (39.5°C) or more, pale gums, or lethargy
- vomits and appears lethargic, attempts to urinate frequently, and has a temperature of 103.5°F (39.5°C) or more, and/or bloody stools

- has diarrhea, bloody feces, an elevated temperature, or is vomiting
- is constipated and strains at the stool while failing to defecate.

Call your vet for advice and an appointment if your cat:

- has abnormally thin stools and an elevated temperature
- has a temperature between 103.5 and 105°F (39.5–40.6°C) and other signs of illness
- begins drinking more water than usual and urinating excessively, has diarrhea, is lethargic, or has an elevated temperature
- has a decreased appetite and is coughing, vomiting, or has diarrhea
- exhibits general lameness in any leg for more than two days
- develops a swelling that is warm and painful to the touch
- has a runny nose accompanied by lethargy, pus in the eye, or rapid breathing
- has a cough accompanied by an elevated temperature, difficult breathing, and lack of energy
- has foul-smelling breath, is drinking water excessively, eating frequently, urinating frequently, yet appears lethargic
- has diarrhea accompanied by dehydration (A cat is dehydrated if you take a pinch of skin from over its spine between your thumb and forefinger, lift the skin away from its body, and let go of the skin, which then does not spring back immediately into place.)

Cats are fond of little people in many guises.

Preventive Health Care

A study published by the American Veterinary Medical Association (AVMA) in 1988 revealed that 59.5 percent of the cat owners in the United States had sought veterinary care for their animals during the preceding year. This represented a 26-percent increase over the precentage of owners (47.2) who had taken their cats to a veterinarian in 1983, the last year in which the AVMA had collected data prior to its 1987 survey. When the AVMA collected data regarding cats' veterinary care in 1992, the percentage of owners who had taken their cats to a veterinarian the preceding year was 62.4, an increase of only 5 percent over the percentage of owners who had sought veterinary care for their cats in 1987.

The AVMA studies disclose two unfortunate facts about the level of cat health care in the United States: It had not improved significantly between 1987 and 1991, and nearly two out of every five cats in the United States received no medical attention in 1991, not even for an annual booster shot and physical examination.

The AVMA data reminds us of the obligations incumbent upon all cat owners. These obligations include prompt, competent, and kindly medical care when necessary; a safe, clean, comfortable indoor environment; a balanced, nutritious, invigorating diet; a yearly examination and booster shots; and habitual, loving human companionship.

Preventive health care begins with the annual trip to the veterinarian for a thorough physical examination and booster shots. In the basic examination, the veterinarian ruffles a cat's coat to check for softness, sheen, and texture, broken hairs, scales, fleas, flea dirt, and ringworm. The vet may also test for dehydration. In addition, the vet looks into the cat's eyes and ears, examines its teeth, listens to its heart and lungs, then palpates its kidneys and liver. Unless there is a reason why a cat should not receive them, the vet then administers the necessary booster shots.

Young, healthy cats do not need as close or as costly an inspection as might older cats, or cats with complex medical histories. Cats ten years old and more—or cats that have had medical problems in the past—may need additional tests to check for diabetes or to monitor blood chemistry, thyroid level, cholesterol, kidney and liver functions, and other conditions. The final component of a cat's annual checkup is the fecal examination, in which a stool sample is assayed for various models of worms. (See Internal Parasites, following.)

Vaccinations

During gestation, kittens normally inherit immunity against various diseases from their mothers. Thereafter, kittens are usually protected by antibodies in their mothers' milk until they are roughly eight weeks old. Because this passive or inherited immunity interferes with the kittens' ability to produce antibodies, they generally are not vaccinated until they reach eight weeks.

The trick in vaccination science is to stimulate the body's immune defenses without causing disease. Thus, when a kitten is vaccinated, a small quantity of vaccine designed to protect against one or more feline afflictions is introduced into the kitten's bloodstream. Immunization, the desired end product of vaccination, is the process by which the immune system recognizes foreign proteins (or antigens) in a vaccine. Once the immune system recognizes these intruders, it manufactures protective proteins (or antibodies) and white blood cells that ingest and remove foreign material from the body.

That initial disease-fighting response, which is low grade and not entirely effective, begins about five to ten days after a kitten has been vaccinated. A second vaccination, which incites a more vigorous, lasting response, is given three to four weeks later.

Vaccines can be introduced into a kitten's body in one of three ways: intramuscularly, intranasally, or subcutaneously. The choice of vaccine and administration method are influenced by circumstance.

Killed vaccine: A veterinarian confident of obtaining effective immunity by using a killed vaccine, one that cannot cause disease or replicate itself, will generally do so because killed vaccines possess greater stability and offer maximum safety. A veterinarian who suspects that a kitten might be immunosuppressed would also use killed vaccine because it does not contain live virus.

Modified live vaccines: These are chosen when a faster, more broad-based immune-system response is desired. Because modified live viruses continue to replicate in the kitten or cat, they confer a relatively long-term immunity.

Intramuscular or subcutaneous inoculation: A veterinarian using a killed or a modified live vaccine can administer it intramuscularly or subcutaneously. The latter route generally prevails, not because of any physiologic advantage in invoking an immune-system response, but simply because it is more comfortable for the kitten. If for some reason, greater speed of entry into the bloodstream is a factor, intramuscular injection is favored.

Intranasal inoculation: This is an important consideration when it is necessary to vaccinate against the upper respiratory viruses that enter the body through the nasal passages. Intranasal inoculations, which are limited to modified live vaccines, produce a local immune response on the linings of the nasal passages. This response, which can be important in blocking the early phase of infection at the source, may not be produced as readily from systemic vaccination paths.

Most kitten vaccinations are administered in a three-way injection designed to confer immunity against feline panleukopenia, feline viral rhinotracheitis, and feline calicivirus. Fewer than 1 percent of healthy kittens vaccinated in this manner at the proper age with the right dose of a properly stored vaccine will fail to produce an immune response. The same can be said of the rabies vaccine, but not the feline-leukemia-virus vaccine.

Like failure to develop immunity, severe allergic reactions to vaccination are rare. If they occur, the kitten should be taken back to the veterinarian at once. It is a good idea, therefore, to schedule vaccinations for early in the day so that if you have to rush a kitten back to the vet, the office will still be open.

Next to the vaccine, the most important factor in developing immunization is the veterinarian, who by training and experience is best qualified to judge when a kitten is healthy enough to be vaccinated. For this reason, anyone buying a kitten from breeders who give their own shots is foolish for not insisting that the kitten be examined by a veterinarian, preferably before the first vaccination is administered. For no matter how advanced the technology for producing vaccines might become, a vaccination is only as good as the exam that preceded it.

External Parasites

Parasites are living organisms that reside in or on other living organisms (called hosts), feeding on blood, lymph cells, or tissue. Parasites that dwell inside their hosts are called internal parasites (or endoparasites). Those that prowl on the surface of their hosts are called external parasites (or ectoparasites).

The cat's external parasites include fleas, ticks, flies, lice, larvae, and mites. In addition to damaging skin tissue, this motley collection of insects and arachnids may transmit harmful bacteria and menacing viruses to their hosts. In significant quantities, external parasites can leave their hosts devoid of energy, weaken their resistance to infection and disease, and infect them with a number of diseases or parasitic worms.

The presence of external parasites is usually revealed by skin lesions, hair loss, itching, redness, dandruff, scaling, growths of thickened skin, or an unpleasant odor. If any of these symptoms appear, take your cat to the veterinarian for a diagnosis. Cats infected with mites most likely will have to be isolated from other cats and treated with parasiticidal dips, powders, ointments, and shampoos.

Internal Parasites

There are four types of internal parasites that thrive in the cat: protozoa, nematodes, cestodes, and trematodes.

Protozoa: Usually one-celled organisms that may contain specialized structures for feeding and loco-

The life cycle of a tapeworm. The flea, which carries microscopic tapeworm larvae, bites a cat, transmitting the larvae to the cat. The larvae migrate to the intestine, where they develop into a mature tapeworm composed of many flat segments. Each segment absorbs nutrients from the contents of the intestine.

motion, the protozoan most familiar to cat owners is *Toxoplasma gondii*. It can cause retinal lesions, calcified lesions in the brain, which are sometimes fatal, or water in the brain cavity of newborn human infants whose mothers were infected by *Toxoplasma* during pregnancy. Children infected by *Toxoplasma* postnatally may develop a rash, flulike symptoms, heart disease, pneumonia, retinal lesions, and a fatal central-nervous-system infection.

To avoid *Toxoplasma* infection, pregnant women should not clean litter pans, or they should wear disposable rubber gloves if they do. Children, of course, should not be allowed to play near litter pans.

Nematodes: These somewhat resemble earthworms. The nematodes most often troubling to cat owners and their cats are roundworms and hookworms, whose presence can be detected through a stool-sample analysis.

Cestodes (or tapeworms): Not amenable to identification by stool-sample analysis, these worms, which are carried by fleas, are best identified by the ancient Egyptian technique of lifting a cat's tail and peering studiously at its anus. During this examination, the inspector is looking for small, white tapeworm segments that look like reborn stir-fried rice.

Trematodes: These tiny flukes live in the small intestines of their hosts. Because cats generally become infested with trematodes after eating raw fish, frogs, or small rodents—and because conscientious cat owners do not allow their cats outdoors—there is little chance that readers of this text will need to worry about trematodes infecting their cats.

Worms, despite their repugnant aspects, are not difficult to rout. If your cat needs to be dewormed, use a product prescribed by your veterinarian, and be sure to use it according to instructions.

Dental Problems

A cat's teeth should be white and clean, and its breath, while it lacks the freshness of peaches and cream, should not smell like freshly scattered fertilizer either. Cats have 30 adult teeth, which should have replaced and augmented the 26 deciduous or milk teeth by the time a cat is six or seven months old. (Milk teeth begin to appear when a cat is about four weeks old.)

The gums and tissues of a cat's mouth should be pink, except for the black pigment spots that some cats have on their gums. Firm-feeling, pink gums that adhere snugly to a cat's teeth are a sign of good health. Pale gums are a warning that a cat may be bleeding internally or suffering from anemia or any of a number of systemic diseases.

Gingivitis

Gingivitis, whose presence is advertised by a raw-looking, red line in the gums just above the teeth, is a frequent and a stubborn problem in cats. Mild gingivitis may be tolerated by a cat without causing any ill effects. More serious gingivitis is accompanied by drooling and bad breath.

Gingivitis can result from an accumulation of plaque and tartar on a cat's teeth. When plaque spreads beneath the gums, it inflames them, causing redness, swelling, and eventual loosening of the teeth. Gingivitis also can be caused by viruses such as feline calicivirus and feline leukemia virus.

Those owners blessed with patience and with tolerant cats can clean their cats' teeth by rubbing them with a soft cloth (or a cotton swab, a clean finger, a child's toothbrush, or a gauze pad) that has been dipped into dilute hydrogen peroxide, bicarbonate of soda, or salt water. Do not use human toothpaste on your cat.

Whether your cat allows you to "brush" its teeth daily, weekly, or when the moon is new, its teeth should be cleaned professionally at least once a year.

Nursing a Sick Cat

The way a cat sees it, the best thing you can do for it when it is sick is to leave it alone. Cats appreciate and seek the regenerative power of solitude. They expect you to appreciate and respect that power as well. Thus, to nurse a sick cat is to strike a balance between respecting its desire for privacy and helping it to recover.

Not surprisingly, cats do not make the greatest patients. They resist taking pills as though they were being poisoned. They lick any "foreign" material from their coats, especially if it is medicated. They object to being force-fed, and because their instincts tell them they are vulnerable and, therefore, ought to hide when they are sick, they must often be caged in order to be accessible when it is time for 2 A.M. medication.

For these reasons, the seriously ill or injured cat is better left to the ministrations of your vet. Your cat will miss you while it is there, and you will miss your pet, but at least it will not associate you with pills and other unpleasantries.

Lesser ailments and convalescence should be weathered at home in familiar surroundings. This means, of course, that pills and medications must be administered by familiar hands. Namely, yours.

The first principle of home-nursing care is that sick or convalescing cats should be isolated from other cats. The second rule is that persons handling sick or convalescing cats should wash their hands thoroughly and change their clothes before handling other cats. In fact, anyone handling a sick cat would do well to wear rubber gloves. What's more, all bedding, food dishes, water bowls, and litter pans used by any cat suffering from a contagious disease should be disinfected with a nontoxic antiseptic. All leftover food, litter, soiled dressings, excrement, and other waste should be sealed in a plastic bag and placed immediately into an outdoor trash can.

Sick cats are best confined to a double cage, 22 inches (56 cm) deep and tall and 44 inches (112 cm) wide in a warm, quiet, draft-free room. The cage should contain a litter pan, food dish, water bowl, and a cozy cat bed for the patient. Towels around three sides and over the top of the cage may also make your patient feel more secure. Though a cat might not be up to playing with toys, a hanging toy spider in one corner of the cage may eventually prove diverting. If the patient must be kept warm, put a cardboard box, with one side cut down for ease of entry and exit, in one corner of the cage; and put a heating pad covered with a towel in the bottom of the box. Leave a radio, set to an easy-listening or a nonradical talk station, playing softly. Groom the cat as usual if your pet will tolerate it. Otherwise, just hold and pat it gently. Do not spend too much time with it. Sleep is the second-best medicine in most cases.

Because many sick cats are not eager to eat, you will be challenged to concoct something that your cat will find palatable. Forget balanced diets for the moment. Feed a sick cat anything it will eat. Because cats recovering from upper respiratory infections may not be able to smell most foods, use strong-smelling food like sardines or

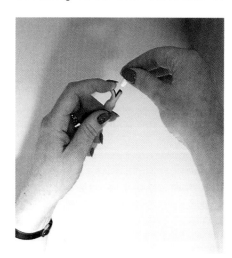

There is more than one way to pill a cat. Pill guns, properly loaded, can help to keep your powder and your fingers dry at medicine time.

tunafish or meat that has been seasoned liberally with garlic. If a cat accepts any of these, you can balance the menu as time passes.

Sliced turkey breast from the deli is a great favorite of sick cats. So is baby food. Some cats will eat a molasseslike, high-calorie food substitute available from your veterinarian.

To make sure that the patient does not become dehydrated, resort to any fluid you have to in order to get it to drink: water, beef broth, chicken broth, or evaporated milk mixed with baby cereal, egg yolk, karo syrup, and a pinch of salt. If your cat is extremely weak, you may have to give it fluids with a plastic eye dropper or preferably a syringe. (See Force-Feeding, page 125.)

Pilling a cat is always a tenuous proposition at best. Some people seem to have been born with a knack for it. They grasp the top of a cat's head in one hand, pinching the corners of its mouth with thumb and middle finger or ring finger to force the mouth open, drop the pill onto the back of the cat's tongue, jab an index finger quickly against the back of its throat, withdraw the finger, hold the cat's mouth shut, then blow quickly into the cat's face to startle it and make it swallow.

Persons lacking this agility and self-confidence resort to pill guns, which still require that someone pry open a cat's mouth to insert the gun, or to hiding ground-up pills in butter, a lump of hamburger, or a mound of baby food. Whatever technique works, praise your cat for taking a pill and give it a treat afterwards.

Force-feeding

Force-feeding is less strenuous on your cat, and your pet's initial resistance may subside when it realizes that the stuff you are insinuating into its mouth tastes good. The technique for force-feeding is similar to that for giving pills. Hold the cat's head from the top. Place your thumb against one corner of the cat's mouth and your middle finger or ring finger against the other corner. Squeeze the cat's mouth open. Put a dollop of food on the index finger of your free hand and rub it onto the roof of your cat's mouth. Relax the pressure on the sides of its face, allowing your cat's mouth to close, but keep its head restrained or else the cat might shake the food out. Putting a small dab of food on the cat's nose, from which it promptly will lick the morsel, is another way of getting your pet to take some nourishment.

If you are feeding liquid foods, put them into a syringe, open the cat's mouth as above, then squeeze some of the liquid into the pocket formed where the cat's upper and lower lips meet. Administer the liquid slowly, allowing the cat time to swallow. Five-cc syringes are easily manipulated. Buy a supply of them and change them frequently.

Skin Medicating

After applying any skin medication, hold your cat or play with it quietly for a few minutes to distract it so that your pet will not lick the medication off at once before it has had a chance to do any good. If skin medication must remain undisturbed for a longer period of time, ask your vet to show you how to fashion an Elizabethan collar that will prevent the cat from licking itself.

When the business of pilling, force-feeding, or medicating your cat is finished, apologize for the intrusion and explain that you are really trying to help. Then sit with your pet quietly for a while, commiserating.

Chapter 11

Professionally Speaking

If a script calls for six cat tricks, find six cats that look alike and train each one to do a separate trick.

Ancient Hollywood Proverb

That proverb is a sound one, says California-based animal trainer Cristie Miele, who specializes in training exotic animals for movies, commercials, and public appearances. Miele works for Animal Actors of Hollywood for whom she has trained monkeys, lions, leopards, wolves, reindeer (in Norway), and cheetahs (in Africa). She also has trained garden-variety domestic cats for films such as *Always, Unlawful Entry, Dennis the Menace, Pet Sematary II, Single White Female,* and others.

"When we supply a cat for a film," says Miele, "we actually supply a team of cats. Each team consists of three or four cats—sometimes more, depending on the project—that look alike. Our main team is a longhaired orange-tabby team. There are four cats in that one, including two brothers. Each cat in the team has a specialty. One is good at staying and lying around. Another is action oriented, running

fast from point A to point B or climbing a tree. Another is good at rubbing against people's legs or hitting a mark."

How Cat Actors Hit Their Marks

Cats have to learn to hit their marks just as other actors do. To accomplish that, Miele explains, "you start by teaching a cat to stay. (See Stay, page 103.) It's easiest to do if the cat is sitting on something. I start teaching a cat to stay on a chair that's 3 feet (91 cm) off the ground. Then I go to a chair that's 1 ½ feet (46 cm) off the ground. From there I go to a chair that's half a foot (15 cm) off the ground. Then I go to the ground. When I do, I might rehearse a cat within a small area set off by pieces of tape. As long as the floor isn't going to be visible in the scene, I can leave the tape there. If not, the cat still knows the general area I want him to remain in."

Besides being trained to stay on a mark, cats can be trained to go to a mark, says Kathryn Segura, who owns and operates PHD Animals in Studio City, California. Segura has trained the lead dog and all the other animals for the television series *Reasonable Doubts* and has supplied many animals for *Rescue 911.* She has located rare breeds of animals for the educational program *Animal Crack-ups.* In addition she has supplied animals for the *Addams Family* movie, *Indecent Proposal,* and the coneheads movie, as well as many others. Several years ago she was asked to provide a cat for a public-service announcement. The cat in the announcement was supposed to emerge from a clump of bushes, jump onto the wall of a small, brick bridge, and walk a dozen feet (4 meters) to where actress Marsha Mason was sitting. Beneath the bridge was a pond in which swam ducks and geese.

All of the cats Segura uses in her work are also her pets. For this job she chose a female Somali [an Abyssinian with long hair] named Amber.

"I took Amber through the routine on a leash first," says Segura. "I showed her exactly what I wanted her to do and where her mark was. I always pattern any animal in a situation like that. I didn't use any food. I just showed her what I wanted her to do and gave her a lot of praise.

"When we were ready to shoot, I placed Amber in the bushes and gave her a "stay" command. Then I

Kathryn Segura with Amber the cat and two of Amber's friends. Segura has trained many domestic and exotic animals for movies and television.

got behind Marsha, out of camera range. Since Amber is trained to come in response to a clicker, the kind you can buy in a toy store (see page 128), I used the clicker to call her. She knew from being patterned that the place where Marsha was sitting was her [Amber's] mark and that was where she was supposed to go. When Amber came out of the bushes and went up to Marsha, I put my hand out, which is the signal for the "stay" command, and Amber stayed with Marsha. Marsha was petting her, which was, in essence, giving her a reward.

"When Marsha first saw the cat, she looked as if she was thinking, 'Oh my God. This is never going to work. I'm going to be here forever.' But it didn't take much rehearsing."

Many trainers teach cats to respond to a buzzer or a bell in addition to a clicker. "Have you ever seen cats in commercials running across a room?" asks Nancy Kobert. "Those cats are just coming to call signals: a clicker being clicked repeatedly or a buzzer or a bell going off. When they come to that sound, they're always rewarded with food. Usually the set is arranged so that the cat can see right where it's going. In a straight-line shot, someone opens an airline kennel out of camera range, and the cat runs straight across the set to the trainer."

Variations on this theme can be used to get a cat to change direction on screen as though he is looking for something. First a trainer sets up two remote-controlled buzzers in different parts of a room or stage set. One of the buzzers might be in back of a couch cushion. The other might be set up behind a wall. When the cat is let out of the carrier, the trainer activates the first buzzer and the cat heads toward the couch. Then the trainer activates the second buzzer behind the wall across the room. The cat stops when he hears the second buzzer, changes direction, and heads across the room.

"We've got one girl who's so good we can move her all around a room with buzzers," says Kobert. "We can send her to the middle of the room, then we can make her turn left or turn right or come back to us."

The Screen Test

Although some cats used in movies and television are pedigreed, the majority of feline actors, like the overwhelming majority of household cats in America, are of no particular particulars. "Just about all our cats were adopted from an animal shelter," says Miele. "When I go to a shelter looking for a cat, I sometimes want a cat with a specific color to match the rest of the team that cat will be part of. If there are several cats of that color available, I look for the outgoing personalities. Any cat that's up against the cage purring and acting happy is comfortable in that situation and is a good prospect for training. I also take along a toy and see if the cat will play. I like to get young adults because their personalities are already set. They're all neutered and spayed because they're easier to work with that way. I don't have a preference for males or females because I don't think either sex is easier to train than the other, although males are sometimes a little more outgoing.

"The other thing I look for in a cat I'm adopting from a shelter is one with an empty food dish, one that's a bottomless pit. Training cats basically involves bribing them with food. Cats that like to eat generally work better, and when one gets full, that's when you need numbers two, three, and four to pull out."

Unlike Miele, Kobert prefers to start working with very young kittens. "If we're training a cat to perform in public or for films, we start with babies," says Kobert. "People who want to train their cats to do a few tricks around the house needn't start with kittens that young, but we start with babies because the hardest thing about cats is traveling with them. Training them to do tricks is easy, but since traveling is the hardest part, we start traveling with them when they are little to get them used to the idea."

Segura gives her cats a travel test before she begins training them. "If you want to use a cat for any kind of movie work or TV, you have to be able to take that cat with you everywhere like you would a dog. Taking a cat to the vet is not a good example because most animals in general hate going to the vet. People call me all the time to say they have this great cat that would be wonderful on TV. My first question is, have you ever taken the cat out. 'Well, to the vet.' No, not to the vet, to the bank or to a friend's home?"

Segura travel-tests a cat by placing it in a secure carrier and taking it for a ride in the car. She stops at a bank, takes the cat out of the carrier, and begins walking toward the bank with the cat held securely in her arms.

"If we make it into the bank and people fuss over the cat and the cat seems fine and relaxed," says Segura, "then he or she will probably be okay on the set." And if the cat begins climbing her face about 10 or 15 steps away from the car, Segura returns the cat to the carrier.

"I don't give up on the cat right away, though" she says. "I'll try again, but if it continues acting stressed, I know it's never going to work outside the house."

Jumping onto a Seat

Some television commercials are preceded by the warning: Do not attempt what you are about to see at home. Teaching a cat to jump onto a seat should contain the same warning. "Once you've taught your kitty that if it jumps onto a stool or seat it's going to do tricks and get food, you may not be able to eat dinner with your cats in the house," laughs Kobert. "We can't because our cats have learned 'if I want food, I go up.' They go up on top of the stove, the counter, the table, and the refrigerator. We have never used the kitchen as a training area, yet we have trouble with every one of our cats. It also could be that I'm a big softy and I'm not tough enough when they jump up there. Maybe I should be more consistent about using a squirt bottle as a negative reinforcer (see Aversive Training, page 79). If you do it consistently, all you have to do is pick up the bottle and they jump down."

Having made that disclaimer, Kobert explains that she begins teaching kittens to jump up onto a seat when they are six weeks old. "Since they're going to be performing out of the house, they need to know that when they see that seat, they should run right over and jump on it.

"There are two schools of thought about teaching a cat to jump onto a stool," Kobert explains. "The purist school says to wait for the behavior to happen, then reinforce it with a reward. In other words, the animal trains itself. You just step in to reward him when what he did was what you wanted. That could take forever. Instead, we use a technique called baiting. We put some food on a spoon or on the end of a blunt piece of dowel. Then we hold the spoon or the dowel in front of the cat's nose and say 'come' or 'here, kitty, kitty.' As soon as the cat follows the food onto the stool, we say 'good' and give it to him.

"We do that over and over. Seat training is important because we travel all over with our cats, and we do a lot of live performances. In a shopping mall, for example, the cats will come out of their crates into a place where they've never been before and everything is unfamiliar. Cats are territorial, and that situation is very difficult for them. Yet if they look up and see their seats, they remember that ever since they were six weeks old that seat has been the place to be, so they hop right up and go to work."

(If you teach a young kitten to jump onto a stool, begin with a stool that is fairly low slung, about a foot (31 cm) high. As your kitten gets older, you will need a higher stool.)

Clicker Training

The clicker training (or buzzer or bell training) used to move cats from one point to another on a movie or commercial set is taught in much the same way as teaching a cat to respond to his name. In fact, if you have taught your cat to respond to his name (see The Name Game, page 90), all you need do is click the clicker immediately before calling your cat's name. After you do this two or three times a day for three or four days, try clicking the clicker by itself. If your cat comes running, he is now clicker trained. If he does not, keep on practicing until he does.

Clicker training can be used for more than calling a cat from across the room. Once Segura was asked to provide a cat for a segment introducing the television show "Funniest Home Videos." The director of this show needed a cat that would look up from its food bowl on cue when "Funniest Home Videos" came onto the screen of a television set in the same room.

"They have a live audience and above the audience is a small stage like a box," says Segura. "It's eight or ten feet above the audience, supported by beams, and it's barely big enough to hold a camera, two small tables, and a few people. They had set up a TV on one table and on the other table, Amber was sitting in front of a food bowl. Before crouching out of camera range beside the TV, I put Amber's favorite wet food in the bowl on her table and gave her a "stay" command. While she was staying, she began eating as she was supposed to do for the script. They told me when to cue her. I told them there was no guarantee Amber would perform because of the audience and all the commotion going on, but she did it in one take. I could not believe it. I was beside the TV table with my clicker. When they said, "action," it was time for her to look up at the television. So I clicked. She looked up. And that was it."

Waving

Dressage is a form of classical riding personified by the famed Lippizzaner stallions. For all of its breathtaking intricacies, this ballet on horseback consists of movements that horses do naturally when gamboling about in the pasture. Like dressage, cat training builds on movements and activities that come naturally to a cat. Indeed, a cat can be trained to do anything it is capable of doing naturally.

Waving is one of those natural tricks. "Once we have taught our cats to jump onto a seat," says Kobert, "the next thing we teach them to do is to wave. That's really easy because it involves one of the cat's natural predatory behaviors: using its feet to grab prey. We use either a spoon or a piece of wooden doweling with food on it. We teach cats to wave by holding the spoon or dowel in front of them. They will try to grab the stick and bring it to their faces because when they hunt, they do the same thing. Once they try to grab the stick, I move it slowly out of reach so that the cat can almost, but not quite, reach it. When the food is just out of reach, the cat will start the wave motion. That's when I say 'good' and give the cat a reward. Eventually, the cat realizes, 'Oh, this is a trick.'"

Kobert stresses the importance of using the word "good" before presenting the reward. "That's called a bridging stimulus, and it tells a cat that what he has just done is the right thing and that he's going to get a reward for doing it. If you don't say 'good' right away, the cat may perform some other random action just before you give him his reward. If so, he's liable to think that's the action he's bring rewarded for.

"When I started training animals, I really blew off the bridging stimulus. I thought, 'He does the trick. I give him the food. That's good enough.' Then I was trying to teach this chicken to turn in a circle. I had set him on a little stool, and he was looking all around, just being a chicken. As soon as he started to make a little movement like he was going to turn to the left, I said 'good' really sharply. The chicken spun around and got the reward. Then I could see him thinking, 'Wow, what did I get rewarded for?' So, he's looking around, looking around, starts to make the turn to the left again, and I say 'good.' Then he gets another reward. It took about four of those before he went, 'Wait a minute, every time I turn that way I hear that sound and then I get rewarded.' That's why it's important to use a bridging stimulus: so what they're really learning is to pair that word with the food reward.

"Training is nothing more than starting a dialogue with a cat. It's like you're working with this little dude from outer space, and you're trying to talk to him. First, you have to have some kind of language."

Walking the Ball

This trick will test your cat's tenacity and yours. In it your cat jumps onto a basketball and makes the ball go forward by moving his feet backward.

"We start teaching this when our cats are little," says Kobert, "because it's a physical trick and it gives us an indication about whether the cat's going to be brave enough to want to do it.

"What's most important with the ball balance is to teach it initially as just a seat. You want to have the cat get onto the ball from one direction, take the food reward, and then get off the ball from the front. If they jump off the ball too soon, I say, 'No. Get on your seat.' I use the dowel over their heads so they'll want to get on the ball. It's important to have the food on the dowel because by controlling the height of the food, I'm controlling the level of the cat's head; and by controlling the level of the cat's head, I can control the way a cat shifts its weight.

"If I want a cat to bring the ball forward, I bring the food down a little bit and the cat lowers his head, too. That causes the ball to roll backward a little and the cat has to move his feet backward to compensate for the movement of the ball in order to stay on top of the ball. If his head comes up too high, he'll tend to shift his weight back and the ball tends to roll forwards, which is dangerous.

"When a cat first starts learning this trick, I set up two pedestals, one on either side of the ball. The pedestals are 3 to 4 inches (8–10 cm) below the top of the ball. So the cat has to step from the first pedestal onto the ball, take the food, and step down onto the second seat. Then he's walked around to do it again. I usually bait him around by saying, 'Come, kitty, kitty, up on the seat, good.' I'm trying to teach him that forward motion. I use my free hand like a training wheel to control the speed of the ball. At first, if I get a cat's head to move down a little bit and the ball goes a quarter of an inch, which causes him to make one little foot go backwards, I say 'good' and make a big payoff. This is a scary trick, but if you do it in teeny baby steps, the cats are not afraid, and it becomes a natural thing that just starts happening."

Retrieving

When most people think of an animal retrieving some object, they usually envision a Labrador retriever or an English springer spaniel sloshing through an autumn afternoon, dead game bird in mouth. Retrieving is not counted among the cat's cardinal virtues. Indeed, if a cat got its mouth around a pheasant, the cat would slink off to a quiet table in the corner to enjoy its good fortune. That is why cats are not as frequently seen on Father's Day cards as are dogs.

But cats can be taught to retrieve a stick, says Miele. You begin by teaching your cat to jump onto a stool about a foot (31 cm) high. She recommends putting the stool and the cat on a table so that you do not have to bend over during the training session. Then show the cat a treat and encourage him to jump onto the stool. As you do, say "seat" because you want him to associate that word with jumping onto the stool. If you work with your cat four or five times a day, about five minutes at a time, he should be jumping onto the seat in a few days because he will have learned that jumping onto the seat gets him all kinds of treats.

"Once you've taught your cat to jump onto the seat, put the seat away," says Miele. "Then get a 'retrieve stick,' a wooden dumbbell that you can buy at a dog show or a pet store. Get the smallest size— the kind people use with a Yorkshire terrier or other toy dog.

"Lay the retrieve stick in front of the cat. When he sniffs it, say 'good' and give him a treat. Because he received a treat for sniffing the stick, the odds are ten to one he's going to sniff it again. When he does, give him another treat. It may take a while for your cat to become interested in the stick, and the first time he sniffs it, it will probably be by chance. So you'll have to be patient.

"Once your cat catches on to the idea that he gets a reward for sniffing the stick, change the routine. When he sniffs the stick, don't reward him. And don't say 'good' either. Soon he will start getting frustrated, and in his frustration he'll probably mouth the stick. (You can try putting the stick into his mouth, but that usually doesn't work. What does help is smearing a little bacon grease or food on the stick to get him interested in biting it.)

"The first time he puts his mouth over the stick, praise him and reward him. Keep rewarding him each time he puts his mouth around the stick. Repeat this routine at least four times a day for a week.

"Once your cat knows to bite onto the stick, bring back the seat. He'll want to jump onto it because he knows he'll be rewarded if he does, so you'll have to restrain him for a moment. Place the stick in his mouth then let him leap onto the stool. The moment he lands say 'good,' and when he drops the stick, pay him his reward. Eventually he will learn that he's supposed to bring the stick with him when he jumps onto the seat.

"Each time you put the stick in your cat's mouth, say 'pick it up.' Before long he will associate these words with having the stick in his mouth. At the same time, begin moving the cat away from the stool—maybe a foot (31 cm) to start. Gradually he will realize, 'Oh! I only get my reward if the stick is in my mouth and I jump onto the stool.' Therefore, he'll take the stick with him when he leaps onto the seat.

"Up to this point you've been placing the stick in the cat's mouth. Now lay the stick in front of him and say 'pick it up.' Because he's learned that he gets a reward,

he'll pick up the stick and jump onto the stool. Finally, start throwing the stick a short distance and saying 'pick it up.' He'll get it and bring it to the stool. Your cat is now a retriever.

"If you want your cat to bring the stick (or whatever else you've thrown) to a specific spot and to put it into your hand instead of jumping up on a stool and dropping it, you'll have to modify the training routine a little, by using a tin pie pan in place of a stool. As you did before, get him interested in the stick by giving him food each time he sniffs it. Eventually (with the help of some bacon grease or food), he'll bite on the stick, and you'll reward him.

"After your cat bites the stick, have him drop it into the pie pan before he gets his treat. (You can make this easier to do if you hold the treat over the pie pan.) Soon the sound of the stick hitting the pan will act as reinforcement, and he will realize that he's got to drop the stick into the pan to get a reward. That's when you start moving him away from the pan. He will want to get to the pan to collect his reward. So you restrain him a moment, putting the stick in his mouth and saying 'pick it up.' As he moves toward the pan with the stick in his mouth, he soon figures out that he must hold the stick until he gets to the pan.

"Once you have moved your cat a little distance from the pan, you can start throwing the stick and telling him to pick it up. Soon he will bring it to the pan. Then try putting your hand over the pan and having him drop the stick into your hand. After a while he won't need the reinforcement of the pan anymore. You'll just toss the stick, say 'pick it up,' and he'll bring it right to you."

Miele estimates that "with four or five short training sessions a day, the average cat will take about four weeks to learn to retrieve a stick. But some cats never learn, so don't be discouraged if yours is one that won't."

If the foregoing sounds complicated, it is. But complications are what separate the professional from the amateur. Complications and attitude, says Kobert. "I think professional trainers have a realistic understanding of their animals' limits and might be more inclined to be patient and analytical," she says. "A lay person sometimes might think, 'You're just doing this to make me look bad' when a cat doesn't do a trick in front of company. A professional trainer views an animal as an animal and respects its natural abilities, its natural instincts, and uses those to (the trainer's) advantage. What I tend to see a little bit more with regular folks is that they take everything personally. So there's probably more potential for disaster with a lay person.

"Cats don't misbehave to spite their owners. They misbehave because they're animals and we make them live in a house. I love having my kitties in the house, but I also know that they do scratch the furniture because they're scent marking, they do like to get into food if it's available, and they will eat the parakeet if the parakeet gets out. The professional respects that. A lay person might say, 'Oh, my Boots just wouldn't eat Tweedy because he knows how much I love Tweedy.' People who treat their animals like children sometimes forget that a cat is an animal, and they miss an opportunity to be with a neat creature when they don't treat it like what it really is."

The cat on the left demonstrates a scientific principle: Cats abhor empty baskets. Meanwhile, the ears of the cat on the right are of such magnitude that it looks as though it could have been on the other end of the line when E.T. phoned home.

Bibliography

Carlson, Delbert G., DVM, and Giffin, James M., MD. *Cat Owner's Veterinary Handbook.* New York: Howell Book House, 1983.

Fogle, Bruce. *The Cat's Mind: Understanding Your Cat's Behavior.* New York: Howell Book House, 1992.

Fox, Michael W. *Inhumane Society: The American Way of Exploiting Animals.* New York: St. Martin's Press, 1990.

Mery, Dr. F. *The Life, History and Magic of the Cat.* New York: Grossett & Dunlap, 1968.

Natoli, Eugenia. *Cats of the World.* New York: Crescent Books, 1987.

Necker, Claire. *The Natural History of Cats.* South Brunswick and New York: A.S. Barnes and Company, 1970.

Repplier, Agnes. *The Fireside Sphynx.* New York: Houghton Mifflin & Company, 1901.

Tabor, Roger. *The Wild Life of the Domestic Cat.* London: Arrow Books Limited, 1983.

Turner, Dennis C. and Bateson, Patrick, eds. *The Domestic Cat: the Biology of its Behavior.* Cambridge, England: Cambridge University Press, 1988.

Zeuner, F.E. *A History of Domesticated Animals.* New York: Harper & Row, 1963.

Index